D0991073

# THE WORK/LEISURE TRADE-OFF

# THE WORK/LEISURE TRADE OFF

Reduced Work Time
for Managers and
Professionals

## Ann Harriman

BOWLING GREEN STATE UNIVERSITY
DISCARDED
LIBRARY

PRAEGER

PRAEGER SPECIAL STUDIES • PRAEGER SCIENTIFIC

Bowling Green Univ. Library

Library of Congress Cataloging in Publication Data
Harriman, Ann.
  The work/leisure trade-off.

  Bibliography: p.
  Includes index.
  1. Part-time employment.   2. Profesional
employees.   3. Middle managers.   I. Title.
HD5110.H35          331.25′72          81-17782
ISBN 0-03-058966-5                     AACR2

Published in 1982 by Praeger Publishers
CBS Educational and Professional Publishing
a Division of CBS Inc.
521 Fifth Avenue, New York, New York 10175 U.S.A.

© 1982 by Praeger Publishers

*All rights reserved*

23456789   145   987654321

Printed in the United States of America

To Ann Lyall Hutcheon

Mentor, Model, Mother, and Friend

# ACKNOWLEDGMENTS

No scholarly effort is ever a single-person undertaking, and this one is no exception. A debt of gratitude is owed to many people and organizations, and only a few of them can be acknowledged here.

The National Association of Schools of Public Administration and Affairs (NASPAA) and the National Association of Counties (NACo) provided financial support for the original research through a Public Personnel Management Research Fellowship. Additional support was provided through two grants from the Faculty Development Fund of the California State University and Colleges.

The interviewees gave unstintingly from their precious stock of time. A promise of confidentiality precludes me from naming them here; each of them understands how much he or she contributed to the outcome. They are an exceptional group of people. It was a rare privilege to have the opportunity to get to know them.

A whole network of people interested in the broad range of alternative work patterns has been an important source of both information and encouragement: Bob Rosenberg at the California Senate Office of Research; Barney Olmsted and the entire staff at New Ways to Work; Fred Best at California Department of Employment Development; Marian Honeycutt at California State Personnel Board; Ellen Russell at the Federal Office of Personnel Management; Carla Katz at Pacific Telephone; Rosemary Mans at Bank of America; and many, many more.

Lyn Delapp, in whom I like to see a younger version of myself, has provided essentially keen insights and observations. It is because of Lyn and others like her that organizational and social change becomes a vital and dynamic issue.

Margo Britton combines the best of the traditional work values with a sophisticated knowledge of the intricacies of modern word processing. Her skill, combined with her patience and understanding, has been invaluable.

Diane Paige and Jack Stockman, faculty colleagues and friends, have been particularly helpful and encouraging—always willing to share a new resource, review a new idea, or offer a careful critique.

Family and friends who understand why I have to work such long hours to complete a book on reduced work time—or who sometimes don't understand but forgive me anyway—are my special joy in life.

To all of these, and to all the others who have contributed in some way to this effort, goes my heartfelt appreciation. I freely acknowledge their contributions while at the same time, of course, reserving for myself whatever accountability is necessary for errors in fact or interpretation.

# FOREWORD
## Patricia Schroeder
## U.S. House of Representatives

The standard 8-hour day and the 40-hour week were won in the 1930s by union strength and legislation. This was a tremendous step forward from the more extended hours worked in the early 1900s.

Today we are faced with a different scenario. Changes in the family, economic conditions, and life styles have made employees interested in having more choice over their work schedules. Employers have also learned that they can reap benefits from greater utilization of alternative work schedules.

In 1978, when I chaired a House civil service subcommittee, we enacted two bills to promote these changes in the Federal workforce. The Federal Employees Part-Time Career Employment Act, P.L. 95-437, required Federal agencies to establish part-time hiring programs, provided part-time employees with fringe benefits that were proportional with their hours worked, and specified that part-time workers be counted by full-time equivalents—a fraction of a full-time slot—for purposes of the Office of Management and Budget's agency personnel ceilings. Although there was some management resistance to part-time hiring, the numbers of permanent part-time employees increased by almost 10,000 during the first 30 months following enactment of the law. Thirty percent of these part-timers converted from full-time Federal jobs.

The Federal Employees Flexible and Compressed Work Schedules Act, P.L. 95-390, established a three-year experiment in the Federal government for agencies that wanted to establish flexitime or compressed work week programs. For the duration of the experiment, overtime legislation was waived to permit employees to work four 10-hour days without being paid overtime. The legislation required that compressed work schedules be negotiated with the employee organizations. The program was deemed a success, with some 347,000 Federal employees working a compressed work week, and more than one million using flexible work schedules, within the regular 40-hour week.

More recently, I have introduced the Short-Time Compensation Act of 1981 to encourage states to amend their unemployment compensation statutes to permit payment of unemployment insurance benefits to workers who are partially laid off. This legislation would give employers an alternative to the current policy of laying off "the last hired," who are usually minorities, women, and younger workers, during economic downturns. It would require approval of the union before work sharing could be adopted. California was the first state to institute a shared work-U.I. program, and it has been judged successful by employees, employers, and unions in that state.

The relationship between voluntary, flexible reduced work-time options and the increase in the number of two-paycheck families is clear. Increased inflation has made it necessary for couples to have two paychecks to keep pace with the rising cost of living—leaving them with too little time for family and leisure. With a voluntary, flexible reduced work-time program they might choose anything from a shorter work day, fewer days per week, or occasional mini-vacations to coincide with school vacations, or even a longer vacation. At the same time, those who need a full salary can continue to work a standard schedule and, in some cases, to work overtime.

Carried a step further, a voluntary, flexible reduced work-time program might include a multi-year arrangement where an employee could "bank" reduced work-time credits for a sabbatical leave—for travel, education, or maternity or paternity leave.

Rigid work schedules cause workers to leave the labor market. For example, voluntary reduced work-time schedules can help handicapped workers, women during pregnancy, or older workers who would prefer phased retirement. Technological advances, particularly the micro-processor, will induce widespread changes in the way work is organized. Among other things, they free the worker and the employer from time and space constraints, making it possible for significant amounts of work to be done outside of the normal working hours and away from the employer's primary place of business. Some companies are already experimenting with "flexi-place" to allow employees to do a portion of their work at home. This affects traffic congestion, energy use, and urban housing.

I am not suggesting that voluntary reduced work-time is the cure for the common cold or that all of these problems will be solved overnight. But I am suggesting that freeing the work place from standard, rigid time and pay schedules is consistent with the world we live in now and can benefit both employees and employers.

# CONTENTS

PART II

# THE WORK/LEISURE
# TRADE-OFF

# 1

## IT'S ABOUT TIME

> There's a time for some things, and a time for all
> things; a time for great things, and a time for small
> things.
>
> Cervantes

This book is about time. It's about "Time" and "Life." It's
about how job time and leisure time are allocated <u>by</u> us and <u>for</u> us
in contemporary society. It's about the way our lives, individually
and collectively, are affected by that system of allocation of time.

On the one hand, it's about a major paradigm shift. It's about
major social and technological changes that have occurred and are
occurring. It's about the way we produce wealth and the way we
distribute it. Mostly it's about some individuals and organizations
that have deviated, however slightly, from a system of rigid and
inflexible time allocation.

On the other hand, it's about a very simple idea, a minor
adaptation of normal organizational procedures. Job design typically starts with the assumption that the employee will work 40
hours per week, that the tasks required can be divided into five
eight-hour segments, and that the employee can and will adjust his
or her personal life to fit that schedule. This book suggests that
that procedure might be challenged, that the starting point might
be the requirements of the job itself <u>and</u> the preferences of the
employee. The schedule then follows the constraints of the job and
the job holder, rather than the reverse.

The issue is, of course, not quite that simple. Many employees, given the choice, would opt for not only a <u>flexible</u> schedule
but also a <u>reduced</u> schedule. Many will choose to trade some

portion of either their present income or future pay raises for additional time away from the job, particularly if they can choose when
to take the additional time off [1]—so we are talking not only about the
arrangement of time but also about the amount of time that an employee devotes to his or her job and about how <u>that</u> time is arranged.

We will argue that replacing rigid and inflexible schedules
with voluntary and flexible ones makes sense organizationally,
technologically, and socially.

Further, we will argue that <u>it's about time</u>!

## TIME AS A COMMODITY

This entire discussion, it should be noted, is based upon a
particular perception of time, one that differs from the perceptions
of time found in other societies or other cultures. Robert Graham
has identified three concepts of time to illustrate the difference between our perceptions of time and those of other cultures. [2] He
calls them linear-separable, circular-traditional, and procedural-
traditional.

### Linear-Separable Time

In the Western, or "Anglo," perception, time occurs linearly;
it has a past, a present, and a future. It is separable into various
discrete compartments—it can be sliced, chopped, or allocated for
specific purposes or tasks. This conception looks upon time as a
commodity; hence we often use a money metaphor when speaking
about time—time can be saved, spent, or wasted. If we are very
clever we can even buy time. Because it is a commodity, we can
allocate it; we can choose how to spend it. Also because it is a
commodity, we can maximize it. It has a marginal utility, and we
seek to maximize our utility.

Time in this sense has a heavy future orientation. We plan;
we look ahead. Present activities are looked upon not so much as
ends in themselves but as means to accomplish some future goal.
We often think and speak of time and money almost synonymously.
We say, "Time is money," but we also tend to think and act as if
money is time.

### Circular-Traditional Time

Some traditional cultures tend to perceive time in a cyclical
pattern rather than linearly. Actions are regulated not by the clock

but by some natural patterns—the tides, the sun and moon, the seasons. Life, and life's events, tend to be organized around food cycles—agriculture, food gathering, or hunting, depending on the source of food supply. Since these cycles occur in nature, without any human intervention, the expectation is that the future will be very much like the past; therefore, the emphasis tends to be on the present. Time is not planned, it is not segmented, it is not allocated. Events or activities tend to be carried on simultaneously, and everything may take a great deal longer than in a linear-time framework. Time is not a commodity, nor is it a consumer good. It is not money.

## Procedural-Traditional Time

In some traditional societies, notably those with little or no written history, procedure, that is, doing things correctly, becomes the important variable in any activity. Cultural traditions are passed on by ritual, by procedure, and the notion of limiting them by time would seem ridiculous, even outrageous. Time and money are disjoint concepts, and members of the society would be unable to grasp the notion that there is a relationship between them. As in the circular-traditional culture, the emphasis is on tradition, on the present rather than the future. It is important that things be done right, correctly—rather than "on time."

## WHOLE TIME VERSUS PART TIME

No one would argue with the assertion that Western cultures embody a linear-separable perception of time. That perception, in turn, translates into a lifetime segmentation of roles—early childhood, education, work, and leisure (retirement).[3] At each step except the last we are anticipating the next, deferring present gratification for the promise of future rewards.

Complex organizations also adopt policies and practices that assume a linear-separable perception of time. At least up until very recently, contemporary society has not only segmented time; it has also segregated the roles of men and women in the society. Men, the breadwinners, have had their lives and their time regulated by these organizational constraints. Women, however, to the extent that their domain has been the home and family, have also had to adapt to a circular-traditional perception of time. In the long run, biological clocks regulate the time for marriage, child-bearing, and child rearing. In the short run, they regulate the time to eat and to sleep. The seasons affect the weather, and the weather imposes its own requirements on those who nurture. To be sure, many of those areas are regulated and regulatable. The point is that these constraints are imposed by nature, rather than by an external force.

One could also argue that, to the extent that women are the keepers of the family's cultural and ethnic traditions, they also adopt a procedural-traditional perception of time. How the family celebrates its holidays, how it rejoices over the triumphs of its members, how it mourns its failures and losses—in short, the whole cultural fabric that holds the family together—often is determined primarily by the wife and mother. To the extent that these rituals exist and are valued by the family, they impose a procedural-traditional perception of time on the woman.

Yet the institutions of the society make no allowances for alternative conceptions of time. They impose rigid and standard time schedules on all. As role segregation begins to erode, as women increasingly hold paid jobs and men increasingly share in responsibility for the family, the conflicts between "Anglo" perceptions of time and more traditional perceptions increase.

None of this discussion, however, negates the basic premise that our society holds a commodity view of time. On the contrary, it emphasizes the fact that time is a scarce resource and one that is becoming increasingly scarce.

The Allocation of Time

Over the last century, the amount of time spent on market work has decreased in two senses. First, the percentage of the average male's lifetime spent in the labor market has declined substantially. Because we now spend longer in school, retire at a somewhat earlier age, and live longer, the ratio of work years to nonwork years is smaller; work time is increasingly compressed into the middle years of life. As this has occurred, the linear pattern of lifetime allocations—school, work, leisure—has become increasingly pronounced. [4]

Second, daily and weekly hours spent on the job have declined. [5] Between 1900 and 1948, the average work week decreased from 58 hours to just under 42. Since the 1940s the long-range trend to shorter hours has leveled off. Between 1948 and 1977 the average declined only to 38.5, and most of that decline is accounted for by the increased number of women and students working part time. The average work week for nonstudent males declined only a fraction, from 40.6 to 40.3 hours. These figures, however, exclude increases in holiday and vacation pay, which have risen steadily and by substantial amounts, particularly where there is a collective-bargaining agreement.[6]

The reasons for the leveling off of the downward trend line for hours of work are complex and probably would add nothing to this discussion. The important issue here is that, despite changes in the weekly or yearly or total portion of our lives devoted to a job, we continue to allocate our time in a linear mode. Further, social and organizational policies that require a rigid and standard schedule both assume and reinforce this mode of allocation. Only recently have alternative work patterns received serious consideration.

Full-time/Part-time/Overtime Work

One alternative work pattern that is often proposed is permanent part-time jobs. While for many workers permanent part-time work would alleviate many time pressures, it is a limited solution. The Fair Labor Standards Act of 1938 established the standard work week as 40 hours and provided that anything beyond that would be considered overtime. As a result, anything less than 40 hours a week has come to be considered part-time. One would expect, perhaps, that these terms would be seen as stages of a continuum, but unfortunately that is not the case. While overtime may be an extension of full-time, part-time and full-time are perceived as dichotomous, even when the difference in hours is very slight. The following are aspects of that dichotomy:

1. Full-time workers (especially males) tend to be perceived as breadwinners or at least as self-supporting. Part-time workers may be assumed to be dependent on a breadwinner.

2. Full-time workers are assumed to be permanent members of the organization; part-time workers are assumed to be temporary.

3. Full-time workers are expected to be responsible, productive, and committed. Part-time workers may be expected to be irresponsible and unreliable.

4. A healthy adult male will always be assumed to be a full-time worker. It is assumed that part-time workers are women, students, the elderly, or the handicapped.

5. Full-time workers are normally found at every level of the organizational hierarchy and in every job classification. Part-time workers are normally found in only the lowest and most menial positions.

6. Full-time workers may be eligible for promotion or upward mobility; part-time workers are rarely considered for advancement.

7. Full-time workers are normally eligible for whatever fringe benefits the organization offers; part-time workers may not be. They _may_ receive vacation and holiday pay; they are a good deal less likely to receive health insurance, life insurance, retirement, or profit-sharing benefits. [7]

8. In the event of a lay-off, full-time workers often receive the benefits of seniority. Part-time workers are often the first to be laid off.

9. Full-time workers represent the mainstream of the organization—an important resource. Part-time workers are often considered marginal workers.

Stereotypes often have a basis in reality, and this one is no exception. Of the 13 million part-time workers in the United States in 1977, 81 percent were either adult women or teenagers. [8] Among these women, four out of ten were concentrated in clerical, sales, or other predominantly female occupations. A profile of the typical part-time worker would show a married woman whose husband is employed full-time, who has school-age children, who is a high school graduate, and who works in a white-collar occupation.

Such a worker earns about four-fifths of the full-time worker's pay and usually earns fewer fringe benefits as well. The disparity among earnings varies greatly from industry to industry. The greatest differential occurs in industries that tend to hire a few women and in industries and occupations not usually covered by a union contract. Women who work in unionized industries earn about 40 percent more per hour than women who work in nonunion industries. For part-time employees, however, women who work in unionized industries earn 50 percent more than women working in nonunion activities.

Although increasing proportions of women who are looking for work are seeking part-time employment, few are able to find secure and steady employment. Women part-time workers are unemployed more frequently and for shorter periods of time than their full-time counterparts, and they have a much higher probability of leaving the labor force, whether they are employed or unemployed. Leon and Bednarzik conclude that "it appears that women wanting part-time work test the job market and, if not quickly successful, leave the labor force."[9] Perhaps these women test the market, discover that it offers a relatively small number of jobs in female-dominated occupations, paying 30 percent to 50 percent less per hour than similar full-time jobs; these in turn, pay up to 40 percent less per hour than male-dominated occupations. If they decide to leave this labor market, it should not come as too great a surprise. Realistically, the alternative to full-time work may really be empty time, rather than part-time work.

While women of all ages are seeking part-time work in increasing numbers, the increase in the number of men working part time in recent years can be accounted for almost entirely by a rise in the number of older men (age 60 and up) working part time.10 Men leave the full-time labor force for two reasons: chronic health problems and the increasing financial ability to retire early. Many older men with health limitations would apparently accept part-time work if the opportunities were available; but just as in the case of women workers, male-dominated occupations show a lack of part-time opportunities, which affects managers, administrators, craft workers, and operatives. Just as for the women, sales and service occupations have the highest incidence of older men working part time, while self-employed men in the 60-to-64 age group are two and a half times as likely as wage and salaried employees to work part time.

It is clear that the stereotype of part-time workers has a basis in reality. Half of all part-time workers are women. They work largely in service industries, performing clerical and sales jobs; they are paid significantly less than their male counterparts; and the supply of workers seeking part-time work in these occupations greatly exceeds the demand. Any increase in the number of men working part time is accounted for by older men leaving the full-time labor force because of either physical problems or retirement.

Given this very negative stereotype of part-time workers and the gloomy picture of the labor market for part-time workers, it's not surprising that the number of professional and managerial employees seeking the chance to work part time is small indeed. Evidence suggests, however, that a significant number of these workers—full-time, career-directed, professional, and managerial employees, both male and female—would, given the opportunity, exchange some portion of their present or future income for the chance to spend fewer hours at the job.

Preferences for Time/Income Trade-off

The issue of what work schedules or income levels individuals would choose, and under what circumstances they would make a given choice, is a complex one. A number of surveys have questioned full-time employees about their interest in working part time.11 These surveys suggest that a small but significant number of employees would take advantage of such an opportunity given certain conditions, such as job security and protection of fringe benefits. It is more difficult, unfortunately, to survey individuals who are not now in the labor force to determine what proportion of them would enter the labor force if the requirement to work a standard or rigid schedule were removed.

Economists, of course, have long been concerned with preferences for income, leisure, and "free time." There is an extensive body of theoretical and empirical knowledge that attempts to explain and predict market behavior under a wide range of circumstances.[12] Valuable and informative as these analyses are, they tell us relatively little about individual preferences.

One survey of interest was conducted in 1978 by Louis Harris and Associates.[13] The respondents, a nationally representative sample of the population over 17 years of age, were asked to choose, in a variety of paired choices, between time and money. For example, they were asked to choose between a 2 percent increase in pay and five additional days of vacation pay; a 2 percent pay raise and 50 minutes off one day per week, and so on. The results of the poll suggest that American workers may be interested in forgoing substantial portions of current and potential income for additional time, but that the scheduling of the gain in time is critical to the decision.

When given a choice of a 2 percent pay raise or one of five alternatives for time, only 35 percent chose a pay raise. The other 65 percent chose one of the time alternatives; 28 percent chose five additional days of vacation. The other alternatives, in descending order of popularity, were a 50-minute reduction of one work day a week, earlier retirement, and a ten-minute reduction of each work day. When one choice was a 10 percent pay raise, 29 percent were willing to forgo all of the pay raise for an additional 25 nonwork days. Only 16 percent of the respondents said they would forgo no part of a 10 percent raise for additional nonwork time.

When the questions concerned willingness to exchange current rather than future raises, the responses were more varied. A majority of respondents indicated that they would exchange no part of current income for additional nonwork time, but significant minorities, in fact, did indicate such a desire. Again, the greatest preferences were for time in large blocks—shorter work years— rather than shorter days or shorter weeks. Forty-two percent were willing to exchange some pay for additional paid vacation; another 42 percent would exchange current pay for a sabbatical leave.

A detailed statistical analysis of the responses to the survey is beyond the scope of this work. What is of interest here is the conclusion that a very significant portion of the working population is willing to exchange some portion of income for additional nonwork time. As one might expect, parents in dual-career families, individuals in higher income brackets, and women tended to express

greater than average desire for additional nonwork time. Contrary
to expectations, men had an even greater desire than women to
exchange earnings for additional vacation time. Differences between major social groups were not dramatic, and in every subgroup of the sample—with breakdowns, according to age, gender,
income, social class, and occupations—substantial interest in more
free time was exhibited.[14]   Given the opportunity, many workers
would allocate their time according to a formula different from the
one imposed by their employers.  They would substitute nonmarket
time for market time.  They would substitute time for money.

Reduced Work Time

     This book, then, is about time—not part-time, not full-time,
but whole time.  It's about workers, professional and managerial
employees with an investment in their careers, who choose to
divide their time in some way other than the rigid and standard
forms that have become common practice in recent years.  These
workers have chosen, and have found a way, to change the balance
in their lives—the balance of market time, family life, and leisure.
Some will argue that they are a highly privileged group, and so they
are.  They are privileged in the conventional sense of the word.
For the most part they are bright, educated, attractive, healthy,
successful.  Some of them are also privileged in a more specialized sense; they have achieved a degree of personal freedom that
is rare, indeed.
     Part I of the book lays the groundwork for the study.  Chapters
2 and 3 look at the issue of voluntary, flexible reduced work-time
options from the standpoint of public policy, first as an employment
policy issue, and second as a family policy issue.  Chapter 4 looks
at extant organizational theory in the light of changing social values
concerning work and leisure.
     Part II presents the results of a study of voluntary reduced
work time at both organizational and individual levels of analysis.
Chapters 5, 6, and 7 report on the experiences of a group of professional or managerial employees, from both public- and private-
sector organizations, who have deviated from the standard work
schedule in their organizations.  Chapter 8 addresses the specific
concerns of management in implementing a reduced work-time policy.
     In the concluding chapter, some reflections are offered on
the desirability of pursuing voluntary, flexible reduced work-time
options.

TERMS AND TERMINOLOGY

While this work involves no technical or esoteric language, some of the words used in common parlance take on different meanings in different contexts. What follows is a brief glossary of these words as they are used here.

Voluntary reduced work time: Any program or policy that allows an employee to trade income for nonwork time voluntarily. The employee retains full rank and seniority in the organization. Income is adjusted only in proportion to the reduction in time.

Shorter work week: Any schedule that includes at least one full day off in the standard work week.

Shorter work days: Less than eight hours a day.

Shorter work years: Any of a number of possible schedules, such as occasional scheduled days off throughout the year, one or more weeks of time in a block, alternating weeks or months, or even alternating half years—six months full-time and six months off.

Alternative work patterns: Any of several schemes to vary the standard and rigid work schedules, including compressed work weeks, flexitime, and job sharing.[15] Compressed work-time options reduce the number of days of work but not the number of hours; for example, 4/40 (ten hours a day, four days a week) or 9/80 (80 hours of work in nine working days). Flexitime also rearranges the hours of full-time work. A number of variations of flexitime or glide time are possible. Most plans allow the employee some choice of starting time and ending time each day and include some core time when everyone must be present. See job sharing, below.

Job sharing: Usually refers to the situation in which each of two people works half time, using any of the above schedule options.[16] Job sharing may involve either pairing or splitting. Pairing involves two people with equivalent skills who divide one job. The job holders usually divide the time so that the work station is covered at all times, share the same physical facilities, and work on the same tasks. Pairers will often cover for each other during absences for training, vacation, or sick leave.

Splitting involves dividing one budgeted position into two half-time jobs. Each sharer works on separate tasks or responsibilities. The sharers may or may not share facilities, and they work essentially independent schedules. A variant of splitting is the split-level division, in which a job is divided into higher and lower skill levels, and the tasks, hours, and pay are divided between two employees.

Job sharing can, of course, involve something other than an even
distribution of time. Sometimes, for instance, the sharers will
adopt a 3/5 + 2/5 schedule (in which one sharer works three out
of five days and the other two out of five). Also, job-sharing
arrangements can be developed that involve multiple positions:
for example, six people may share five jobs, each taking a one-
sixth reduction in pay and two months' leave. This form is
sometimes called rotational job sharing.
Work sharing: involves across-the-board, involuntary reduction of
pay and time as an alternative to a lay-off.[17] While collective
bargaining agreements frequently contain work-sharing clauses,
they have rarely been implemented because of the restrictions of
unemployment insurance laws. California is now experimenting
with a work-sharing, short-term unemployment law that permits
employees on work-sharing plans to draw partial unemployment
insurance.[18]
Leisure sharing: A proposal to encourage voluntary reduced work-
time programs as an approach to problems of chronic high unemployment.[19] While work sharing addresses problems of
cyclical unemployment, leisure sharing is concerned with secular unemployment. The approach relies on significant numbers
of employees being willing to reduce their work time voluntarily
and also on employers hiring new workers to replace the lost
productive capacity.
Flexible life planning: A concept that challenges the traditional life
cycle of school, work, leisure (retirement).[20] Flexible life
planning (or flexible life scheduling) would encourage the extension of schooling throughout one's lifetime and a more flexible
relationship between job and leisure so that leisure is not relegated to the end of life.
Flexible compensation: Sometimes called smorgasbord compensation or cafeteria benefit plans.[21] Flexible compensation allows
an employee to choose what portion of his or her total compensation package will be taken in salary and what portion in fringe
benefits. It also permits a choice of benefits. Flexible benefits
(or smorgasbord or cafeteria benefits) offer a fixed amount of
salary but allow employees to choose their own benefit packages.
A number of alternatives to these basic models are used in
practice.

Another set of definitions is essential to the ensuing discussion
(particularly in Chapter 4), which rests partly in a distinction among
"work," "labor," and "job," and among "leisure," "free time,"
"play," and "idleness." These words, too, are often used inter-
changeably, causing confusion or misunderstanding.

Work: The set of meaningful activities by which an individual defines himself or herself. Work provides intrinsic rewards; it may or may not be undertaken for pay or other extrinsic rewards. Work is undertaken for its own sake and not because it is prescribed by one's role as job holder or by any other social or family role. It is akin to the notion of a calling or a vocation.

Labor: The set of activities performed either on or off the job that are necessary for maintaining life or livelihood. Labor may or may not be onerous, it may or may not provide extrinsic rewards, and it may require either physical or mental effort. Labor is prescribed by one's roles in the organization, the family, or the society.

Job: The set of activities by which one earns one's livelihood. It is activities and responsibilities undertaken for pay. A job may include both work and labor. It must meet the individual's instrumental need for money and security; it may or may not meet the individual's expressive need to engage in activities that have meaning to the individual.

Career: A set of job sequences that requires a high degree of commitment and investment, in either education or experience, and that has a continuous developmental character. It is a pattern of jobs. It, too, has both limitations and advantages in terms of meeting the individual's instrumental and expressive needs.

Leisure: Like the word work, is used in a variety of contexts with a variety of meanings. Chapter 4 develops a concept of leisure as activities freely undertaken, chosen from among alternatives, and pursued for the personal pleasure and satisfaction that they provide. Leisure excludes activities prescribed by job or role, or that are necessary to compensate for job requirements. It may include activities associated with one's job if such activities are undertaken by choice.

Leisure is distinct from "free time," which sometimes is used to mean all nonjob time and sometimes is limited to discretionary time. It also is distinct from "play," although play activities could be included in leisure. Finally, it is distinct from "idleness," although idleness, too, in the Aristotelian sense of contemplation, can very well be leisure. The distinguishing criteria of leisure are the individual's freedom to choose the activity and the reasons for choosing it.


IT'S ABOUT TIME

This book is about time—work time, job time, labor time, leisure time. It's about balancing and integrating those times of our lives, for our own sakes and for the sake of the social world we live in.

NOTES

1. Fred Best, Flexible Life Scheduling: Breaking the Education-Work-Retirement Lockstep (New York: Praeger Special Studies, 1980).
2. Robert J. Graham, "The Role of Perceptions of Time in Consumer Research," Journal of Consumer Research 7 (March 1981):335-42.
3. Juanita Kreps, Lifetime Allocation of Work and Leisure (Durham, N.C.: Duke University Press, 1971).
4. Fred Best, Exchanging Earnings for Leisure: Findings of an Exploratory National Survey on Work Time Preferences, R & D Monograph 79, U.S. Department of Labor, 1980.
5. John Owen, Working Hours: An Economic Analysis (Lexington, Mass.: Lexington Books, 1979).
6. Best, Flexible Life Scheduling.
7. Bureau of National Affairs, Bulletin to Management No. 1295, "ASPA-BNA Survey No. 25—Part-time and Temporary Employees" (Washington, D.C.: Bureau of National Affairs, 1974), in New Patterns of Work: Highlights of the Literature, ed. Stanley Nollen (Scarsdale, N.Y.: Work in America Institute, 1979).
8. Carol Leon and Robert Bednarzik, "A Profile of Women in Part-time Schedules," Monthly Labor Review 101 (October 1978): 3-12.
9. Ibid.
10. Philip Rones, "Older Men: The Choice Between Work and Retirement," Monthly Labor Review 101 (October 1978):3-10.
11. Stanley Nollen, Brenda Eddy, and Virginia Martin, Permanent Part-time Employment: The Manager's Perspective (New York: Praeger Special Studies, 1978); cf. State of Wisconsin, Project Join: Final Report (Madison, Wisc.: Department of Employment Relations, 1979).
12. Owen, Working Hours; cf. Work Time and Employment, A Special Report to the National Commission for Manpower Policy, Special Report #28, Washington, D.C., October 1978; Gary Becker, "A Theory of the Allocation of Time," The Economic Journal 30, no. 200 (September 1965):493-517.
13. Best, Exchanging Earnings for Leisure.
14. Best, Flexible Life Scheduling.
15. Allen Cohen and Hermon Gadon, Alternative Work Schedules: Integrating Individual and Organizational Needs (Reading, Mass.: Addison-Wesley, 1978).
16. Barney Olmsted, "Job-Sharing: A New Way to Work," Personnel Journal (February 1977):78-81; cf. Barney Olmsted and Suzanne Smith, Job Sharers: Working Less and Enjoying it More, Headlands Press/Penguin, forthcoming.

17.  Sar Levitan and Richard Belous, "Work Sharing Initiatives at Home and Abroad," Monthly Labor Review 100 (Spring 1977): 16-20.

18.  James W. Singer, "Sharing Layoffs and Jobless Benefits: A New Approach is Attracting Interest," National Journal, February 9, 1980, pp. 232-35; cf. Alan Locher, "Short-Time Compensation: A Viable Alternative to Lay-Offs," Personnel Journal (March 1981):213-16.

19.  Leisure Sharing, Hearings of the Select Committee on Investment Priorities and Objectives, California, November 1, 1977.

20.  Life Cycle Planning: New Strategies for Education, Work, and Retirement (Summary of national conference, April 20-22, 1977, Washington, D.C., Center for Policy Process); cf. Best, Flexible Life Scheduling.

21.  "New Life for Flexible Compensation," Dun's Review (September 1978):66-70; cf. "New Tax Law Encourages Companies to Offer Employees 'Menu' of Benefits in Cafeteria Compensation Programs," World of Work Report (February 1979):10-11; cf. James Shea, "Cautions About Cafeteria-Style Benefit Plans," Personnel Journal (January 1981):37, 38, 58.

# PART I

The Concept of
Voluntary, Flexible
Reduced Work Time
for Professionals and
Managers

# 2

## REDUCED WORK TIME AS
## AN EMPLOYMENT POLICY ISSUE

Neither political nor religious doctrines must insist
that everybody work for a living. Every form of government has a doctrine of equality, much as every
religion has. . . . If a doctrine of equality is extended
to work, however, it stunts the growth of a life of leisure. The pursuit of happiness, which . . . originates
as the free and various pursuits of men of leisure,
comes to mean, in the hands of the court, the pursuit
of work. No matter how we come to think of work as
the mark of a free man, in the idea of leisure it becomes prostitution, the bending of mind and body for
hire.

                                  Sebastian de Grazia

Increased opportunities for voluntary, flexible reduced work-
time options have been urged on both economic and social grounds.
As both unemployment and inflation continue to plague the economy,
it becomes increasingly clear that there are no obvious solutions,
nor are their painless ones. Traditional approaches to unemployment center on methods of creating new jobs, that is, increasing
the demand for labor. More recently, attention has turned to the
possibility of using work-sharing or leisure-sharing approaches,
which attempt to decrease the supply of labor. The work-sharing
approaches primarily address cyclical unemployment, affect oper-
ating- or production-level employees, and are not strictly voluntary.
In fact, they may be entirely involuntary. Participants are likely to
be healthy, adult male employees. Leisure-sharing approaches, on
the other hand, address the secular unemployment problems that

currently persist, would be available to employees in all categories, and are voluntary.

As increasing numbers of women enter the labor force, including married women, married women with children, and single women with children, public concern increasingly focuses on problems of the family. Historically, public policy and organizational structures are built on the assumption that workers are males who support a dependent wife and children. Efforts to ease the pressures of two-paycheck families have consistently included proposals for increased use of alternative work schedules—flexitime, compressed work weeks, and permanent part-time work and job sharing. These proposals usually carry with them an assumption that, while male workers might participate in and benefit from a rearranged work week, only female workers—or older workers, the handicapped, or students—would choose to work a reduced schedule.

Very recently, however, discussions of employment policies and compensation programs have included proposals that would allow all employees to exchange some portion of their current or future income for additional nonwork time, in the form of either shorter work weeks or shorter work years. Farther-reaching proposals would allow multiyear accumulations of time, for example, sabbatical leaves, parental or educational leave, early retirement. These approaches offer greater flexibility to both employer and employee than either alternative work schedules or work-sharing plans. Yet they have the potential of addressing the concerns of both manpower policy makers and family policy makers.

Chapter 3 will address the family policy issue. In this chapter, voluntary, flexible reduced work-time options will be shown to be an important element of the public debate on all policies that affect employment. The bases of the argument are:

1. We are firmly committed to an exchange economy, which depends upon continuous economic growth.

2. Despite high levels of unemployment, the economy may be at full employment, making traditional policies ineffective in reducing secular unemployment.

3. While demographic trends may create a labor shortage in the future, developments in electronic technology may bring on widespread unemployment.

4. Existing policies depend to a very large extent both on the assumption of a single earner with dependent spouse and children, and on the assumption of a current definition of the standard work week.

Therefore, policies that encourage employer and employee to consider flexible, voluntary, reduced work-time options may offer a tool for manpower planning by providing a vehicle for expanding or contracting the supply of labor.

## THE EXCHANGE ECONOMY AND ECONOMIC GROWTH

It may be restating the obvious to point out that in contemporary discussions of the allocation of resources and the distribution of wealth in the United States, the pre-eminence of the exchange economy is virtually unchallenged. Economists since Adam Smith have relied on the analysis of the process of exchange, or two-way transfers. In the capitalist system, workers exchange their time (labor) for dollars, which are in turn exchanged in the market for goods and services.

When this market system results in high levels of unemployment, which it inevitably does on a periodic basis, attention turns to a discussion of the appropriate policy to stimulate the growth of the economy without incurring unacceptable levels of inflation. The Keynesians urge tax cuts and deficit spending to stimulate the economy; the monetarists urge a tight control over the money supply and/or small government and laissez-faire policy.

To be sure, the assumptions of exchange and the assumptions of growth have been challenged. As early as the mid-nineteenth century, political economist John Stuart Mill was suggesting the possibility of an equilibrium economy. Earlier economists had concentrated their attention on the process of distribution; Mill pointed out that it was production, rather than distribution, that was the province of economics. The economic laws of production concern nature; they are impersonal and absolute. Once wealth is produced, society can distribute it as it chooses, in accordance with its laws and customs.

Mill believed that eventually the world would reach a stationary level; profits would disappear, and there would be no more growth. Improvement would continue to occur in the distribution of wealth. [1]

A century later John Kenneth Galbraith, in The Affluent Society, pointed out that, apart from the views of Fascist and socialist reformers, the conventional wisdom of economists of the "central tradition" had always been concerned with scarcity. The tools to overcome scarcity were efficient production and economic growth. Under capitalism, economic life contained a high level of insecurity. During the Great Depression, the New Deal notion that

government should intervene to increase aggregate demand and reduce uncertainty came to be included in the conventional wisdom.
When World War II ended, scarcity had virtually disappeared, but
concern for productivity remained high, partly because the myth of
scarcity persisted. Galbraith argued that the appropriate way to
eliminate poverty was through the process of distribution, specifically through education and social programs, rather than through
increasing productivity. [2]

Beginning in the late 1960s and continuing to the present, the
arguments against the inevitability of growth are based not in economics alone, but in the interdisciplinary approach of systems
thinkers. Rather than considering the question of whether growth
is necessary, these writers have been concerned about whether
growth, at least unrestrained and infinite growth, is possible.

Nicholas Georgescu-Roegen used the metaphor of entropy,
from the Second Law of Thermodynamics, to point out that the stock
of natural resources that produce energy is finite, that continual
growth decreases the available stock of nonrecyclable energy, and
that ultimately the human species is threatened. "It is as if the
human species are determined to have a short but exciting life." [3]

An international and interdisciplinary group of scholars that
came to be called the Club of Rome published their work, The Limits to Growth, in 1972. They identified five factors that determine
growth—population, agricultural production, natural resources, industrial production, and pollution—and demonstrated that these factors are growing exponentially, not linearly. Through the use of
computer models they concluded that unless there is a world-wide
commitment to policies that would create a global equilibrium, limits to growth on this planet could be reached within the next 100
years. [4]

Following on the heels of Limits to Growth came E. F.
Schumacher's Small Is Beautiful. While Schumacher was very concerned with the quality of life of individuals—much of his work was
grounded in the example of Gandhi and the Buddhist concept of "right
livelihood"—he was also concerned that modern capital-intensive
technologies were reducing our finite supply of natural resources.
He warned that:

> One of the most fateful errors of our age is the belief
> that the problem of production has been solved. This
> illusion . . . is mainly due to our inability to recog-
> nize that the modern industrial system, with all its
> intellectual sophistication, consumes the very basis
> on which it has been created . . . it lives on irre-
> placeable capital. [5]

So it continues. Kenneth Boulding in Ecodynamics, [6] Kirk-patrick Sale in Human Scale, [7] Theodore Roszak in Person/Planet, [8] James Robertson in The Sane Alternative, [9] and many others have sought to challenge the assumption of the market-centered, growth economy and to warn of the eventual, inevitable consequences of failing to plan for a steady-state economy.

In addition to stating his concern for what he has called "spaceship earth," Kenneth Boulding has questioned economists' preoccupation with the exchange economy. Boulding insists that the grants economy—one-way transfers—now represents a significant and increasingly important element in social life. He believes that grants can be described as gifts or as tribute, according to the motive that inspires them, and that the gift-giving motive predominates. Grants take two forms: explicit grants, such as welfare payments or social security payments; and implicit grants, in the form of structural changes that affect the distribution of wealth, like monopolies, tariffs, and tax policies. [10]

Boulding's thesis is that the number and kind of both explicit and implicit grants are growing rapidly, and that this growth has significance for the allocation of resources and the distribution of wealth. However, as yet, policy discussions have continued to look to the exchange economy as the dominant means of allocation and distribution and to the grants economy as a last-resort remedy when the exchange economy creates unacceptable levels of inequity.

This considerable body of literature challenges the premises of the exchange economy and the significance of growth, yet in practice we continue to pursue policies that are consistent with these premises. The problem we seem to be addressing currently is not the one posed by Mill, Galbraith, or Boulding, of how to improve the distribution of wealth and reduce poverty in a steady-state economy; nor is it the one raised by the Club of Rome of how to preserve life on the planet. Instead, the question being raised is "whether 'tis nobler in the mind" to balance the budget and limit the money supply or to reduce taxes and deregulate and decontrol business. Explicit one-way transfer payments are regarded as inherently evil. It is a measure of the strength of the dedication to the exchange economy that the notion of workfare, that is, turning one-way transfers into two-way transfers, reappears with the regularity and predictability of chain letters.

## THE EXCHANGE ECONOMY AND FULL EMPLOYMENT

There are at least two possible fallacies inherent in the premise that stimulating economic growth will reduce the level of unem-

ployment. The first is that, despite record levels of unemployment
in the last decade, employment has been enjoying a steady rate of
growth. The other is that technological change, primarily the
availability of the microchip and the microprocessor, may mean
that added investment may result in a net loss of jobs.

The unemployment rate in the United States has only twice
slipped below 5 percent since 1970 and has been as high as 8.5 percent (in 1975), clearly an indication of enormous suffering for those
out of work.[11] However, the employment–population ratio, a better
measure of the strength of the economy than the unemployment rate,
indicates that the proportion of the working–age population that is
employed has continued to rise steadily. The overall rate fluctuated
around 55 percent from the late 1940s until the late 1960s. Since
then it has generally risen steadily and now stands at 64 percent.[12]
This analysis leads some economists to conclude that the economy
may already be at full employment, in which case efforts to expand
the economy may increase inflation without materially affecting unemployment.

The question of the impact of technology is also a controversial
one. Any suggestion that automation will result in unemployment is
apt to be met with skepticism, to say the least. Ever since the
Luddites, in nineteenth-century England, smashed machines that
they feared would eliminate the need for their skills, anyone warning about technological unemployment is likely to be labeled a neo-
Luddite. Technology, the counterargument asserts, far from elim-
inating jobs, creates new and more-demanding jobs.

Evidence on technological unemployment is mixed, and there
is some reason to believe that it has, in fact, occurred. There is
no question, however, that technology has brought with it vast social
disruption. Further, the microchip/microprocessor technology differs from past technological advances in some important ways.

Economist Wassily Leontief disagrees with those who argue
that technology has not brought with it widespread unemployment.

> The problem of unemployment cannot be adequately
> posed, not to say solved, without an examination of
> the basic structural characteristics of the modern in-
> dustrial economy, of the position that labor occupies
> within that structure, and in particular, without sys-
> tematic analysis of the decisive change in that position
> brought about by the inexorable forces of the techno-
> logical change. . . .[13]

Leontief compares the argument that workers displaced by machines
will ultimately find better jobs to a proposition that horses replaced

by farm equipment will find work as racehorses. On the other hand, he argues, that same farm equipment, when it is used to replace human labor, increases the income of the farmer and decreases the income of the farm laborer.

Technological change has permitted the reduction of working hours from 70 per week to 40 per week in the past century. Although the rate of decline in working hours substantially decreased some 30 years ago, technological progress has continued and the productivity of labor has continued to rise. Under the influence of cyclical unemployment fluctuations, however, there has been a steady trend toward involuntary nonwork time. Leontief interprets this trend as a sign of a slow but persistent trend toward technological unemployment.

Whether one agrees or not that technological unemployment has occurred in the past, the social upheavals that have resulted from technological advances are undeniable. Jenkins and Sherman, in The Collapse of Work, show that, just as the Luddites had predicted, the Industrial Revolution brought an end to many of the skilled trades and crafts.[14] The steam engine and the consequent move to urban areas brought a breakdown in the traditional family, church, and community values and a concomitant increase in urban problems—slums, pollution, poverty, poor health, and low life expectancy. The development of the internal combustion engine and the motor vehicle brought even more significant changes. The development of mass-production techniques brought cheap transportation to working-class families but resulted in making jobs even more monotonous and repetitious. Further, since the capital outlay for mass-production equipment was so high, it was necessary to operate the machinery 24 hours a day, making shift work a part of the work environment and requiring substantial changes in family and community life.

The electric motor created more jobs than either the steam engine or the internal combustion engine and certainly more than it eliminated. It contributed more, also, to the decline of crafts and the routinization of work.

The computer, the next significant breakthrough in technology, also created great fear for its impact on jobs, but again, it can be argued that more jobs were created by the computer than were eliminated. The early computers required a substantial investment, a large amount of space, and a great deal of highly technical and specialized knowledge. The computer was also relatively inflexible. The result was a marginal increase in the number of jobs, since jobs in installation and in operation outnumbered the jobs replaced. This analysis, however, seems to confirm Leontief's racehorse analogy, unless we can assert that those workers who lost their jobs to computer technology were able to take new jobs in installation and operation.

The advent of the silicon chip and microelectronics constitutes not just an extension of existing technology, but the basis for a third industrial revolution. According to Jenkins and Sherman, this revolution not only will bring about considerable social upheaval but also will cause major unemployment. What distinguishes the microchip and its applications from other new products and applications is that it can be applied in a myriad of ways. It can serve as the basis for a whole panoply of new products—watches, calculators, word processors; it can replace conventional circuitry in existing products; it can change the productive process itself—for example through the development of robotics; and it can affect basic information systems.

The prospects for social change may be alarming or exhilarating, depending on one's point of view. Alvin Toffler, in The Third Wave, predicts that high-technology electronics will permeate every conceivable aspect of our futures. He predicts, with typical Tofflerian hyperbole, a "giant struggle" between defenders of the old order and advocates of the new, with the eventual outcome of "a whole new, more democratic political and social system."[15]

Others may be less grandiose in their rhetoric and more compelling in their effect. The language of high technology is incomprehensible to the uninitiated—microchip, microprocessor, lasers, fiber optics, genetic engineering, artificial intelligence, robotics. Technocrats at a meeting of scientists and engineers in Houston began referring to the neophytes as "Techno/Peasants." The Techno/Peasants then produced a book titled The Techno/Peasants Survival Manual to demystify the technological language and to attempt to demonstrate that these phenomena are "beautifully—and inextricably—mixed."[16] Unquestionably, the possibilities for changing the shape of the social world are no less than awesome.

Is this, though, a real and present danger? Or is it Buck Rogers in the Twenty-First Century? Recently a very large bank, the seventh largest in the United States, reported in the Harvard Business Review on its success in integrating its computer, word-processing, and telecommunications systems so that "executives now have an office wherever there is a phone." Managers can dictate by telephone from any location; various commands such as "record," "play back," or "rewind" can be keyed or dialed on the telephone instrument. Transcribing is done either by community college students working at their campus or by typists working in their homes. The completed work is sent to the bank through the electronic mail system. One-fourth of the bank's employees, about 3,000 people, are included in the bank's electronic mail system and can have access to it from any terminal they choose, again making

location irrelevant. Bank employees who are out of town carry with
them a small computer terminal with which they can retrieve any of
the 20 billion characters of information on file in the system's central library. "Audio Mail" (telephone-answering) devices now take
and give 65 percent of all telephone messages. Managers carry
with them a remote, pocket-size signaling device that permits them
to call the answering machine and get their messages. It appears
to be at least conceivable that an employee could carry out all his
or her assigned tasks without ever seeing or speaking directly to
any other employee.

The authors of the article stress the effect of this electronic
wonderland in freeing employees from specific location. They focus
on issues of job satisfaction, effectiveness, energy conservation,
and productivity. Only implicitly do they consider jobs, but clearly
the productivity increases are a result of more work done by the
machines and less by employees.

> With data processing we had automated the highly
> labor intensive functions of the bank. These included
> check processing, bookkeeping, and other high volume
> arithmetic functions. As technologies improved we ap-
> plied them to word processing—another labor intensive,
> high volume growth segment of the banking industry.[17]

One has to wonder what further technological improvements are
pending and what other labor-intensive, high-volume skills they
will be applied to. Are voice-activated typewriters, perhaps, the
next development?

It is true, of course, that many knowledgeable people reject
the notion that continued economic growth will produce further investment in electronic technology that will reduce, rather than increase, the available supply of jobs. On the contrary, many worry
about a labor shortage in the foreseeable future, based upon demographic predictions.

During the Great Depression and World War II the country's
birth rate was at an all-time low. Those years were followed by
the "baby boom," which lasted up until the early 1960s, when the
birth rate dropped sharply again. Although it has risen slightly in
the late 1970s and early 1980s, it has remained low compared with
the rate during the baby-boom years. As the baby-boom cohort has
moved through the society's institutions, it has caused considerable
upheaval. Consider its effects on employment: the majority of that
cohort is now in the labor market, putting pressure on the system
not only for jobs, but also for upward mobility. Older workers
(aged 55 and above) are, for a variety of reasons, being encouraged

or pressured to leave the labor market and are doing so in substantial numbers.[18] When the baby-boom cohort reaches retirement age, though, and the first of them will be 55 years old in about the year 2000, there will be a much smaller cohort behind them to fill the jobs that they have created.

Another potential problem associated with demographic trends has to do with the problem of redistribution of wealth when the baby-boom cohort reaches retirement age. Early retirements are already reducing the labor-force participation of men 55 and older, and putting strain on retirement and pension systems.[19] According to current predictions, by about the year 2020 there will be only two workers in the labor force for each retired worker, down from the current ratio of five to one. If improved health care continues to add years to average life expectancy, these retirees may prove to be a considerable drain on the society's resources—or, conversely, they may provide a source of scarce labor.

To recapitulate: the United States in the 1980s is firmly committed to an exchange economy, an economy based on two-way transfers. Numerous economists over the years have argued that a steady-state or equilibrium economy is possible and desirable within the confines of this exchange or market-centered economy. Others, the "radical economists," have argued that a steady-state economy is absolutely mandatory for survival. At the same time, some economists are urging, since grants (one-way transfers) are a significant part of our present economy, that economic planning and analysis should include the grants economy as an integral, rather than external, portion of the total economy. Nevertheless, a great deal of the public debate on economic policy continues to assume that unemployment can be solved only by government policies that encourage growth and investment.

There is, however, a question about whether further investment will in fact result in the creation of more jobs. Despite record high levels of unemployment during the last decade, the ratio of employment to population has continued to grow, causing some observers to conclude that we are already at full employment. Further, investment in highly sophisticated electronic technology may substantially increase productivity without increasing the number of jobs. Indeed, some argue that technological unemployment is already occurring and will occur more rapidly as new technologies are created.

These arguments support the proposal that attempting to increase the demand for labor by stimulating investment is not the most appropriate policy. A more appropriate policy would be to decrease the supply of labor by reducing the amount of time spent at work. This policy would encourage employers to adopt work rules or policies that would allow workers to reduce the amount of time spent on the job for a concomitant reduction in pay. Such an approach would include not only shorter work days or work weeks, but also more occasional days off; short vacations; long vacations; sabbatical, educational, or parental leaves; and phased retirements. This approach would encourage shorter work time for all employees who chose to participate, including both women and men, both blue-collar and white-collar workers, both old and young.

An alternative hypothesis holds that in the next several decades we will see a shortage, rather than a surplus, of employees, brought on by demographic changes and the movement toward early retirements. An approach to this problem, ironically, is also reduced work time. The difference is that, in this scheme, reduced work-time options would draw into (or keep in) the work force employees who could provide needed skills but who by preference or necessity do not work full time—the older workers, parents with young children, students, the handicapped. This proposal would attempt to reverse the trend to early retirements by offering phased retirements—a gradual movement from full-time work through reduced time to full retirement.

The great drawback to this second proposal, however, is that it perpetuates the idea of a dual labor market: the healthy adults who are the mainstream of the labor force—the productive core—and the marginal workers who take up the slack—the old, the lame, and the poor. The larger society, as well as individual employers and employees, will be best served by employment policies that support the widest range of choices and the greatest flexibility for all concerned.


NOTES

1. Robert Heilbroner, The Worldly Philosophers: The Lives, Times, and Ideas of the Great Economic Thinkers (New York: Simon and Schuster, 1953); see also Leonard Silk, The Economists (New York: Basic Books, 1976).

2. John Kenneth Galbraith, The Affluent Society (Boston: Houghton Mifflin, 1958).

3. Nicholas Georgescu-Roegen, "The Entropy Law and the Economic Problem," in Toward a Steady State Economy, ed. Herman Daly (San Francisco: W. H. Freeman, 1973).

4. Donella Meadows, Dennis Meadows, Jorgen Randers, and William Behrens III, The Limits to Growth (New York: The New American Library, 1972).

5.  E. F. Schumacher, Small Is Beautiful: Economics as if People Mattered (New York: Harper & Row, 1972).

6.  Kenneth Boulding, Ecodynamics (Beverly Hills: Sage Publications, 1978).

7.  Kirkpatrick Sale, Human Scale (New York: Coward, McCann, and Geoghegan, 1980).

8.  Theodore Roszak, Person/Planet: The Creative Disintegration of Industrial Society (New York: Anchor Books, 1979).

9.  James Robertson, The Sane Alternative: A Choice of Futures (St. Paul, Minn.: River Basin, 1978).

10.  Kenneth Boulding, The Economy of Love and Fear (Belmont, Calif.: Wadsworth, 1972); cf. Kenneth Boulding and Martin Pfaff, eds., Redistribution to the Rich and the Poor (Belmont, Calif.: Wadsworth, 1972); Lester Thurow, The Zero Sum Society: Distribution and the Possibilities of Economic Change (New York: Basic Books, 1980).

11.  "Unemployment Data from the Household Survey," Monthly Labor Review 104 (July 1981): 59.

12.  Carol Boyd Leon, "The Employment-Population Ratio: Its Value in Labor Force Analysis," Monthly Labor Review 104 (February 1981): 36-45.

13.  Wassily Leontief, "Worksharing, Unemployment, and Economic Growth," in Work, Time, and Employment, A Special Report to the National Commission for Manpower Policy, Special Report #28, October 1978.

14.  Clive Jenkins and Barrie Sherman, The Collapse of Work (London: Eyre Methuen, 1979).

15.  Alvin Toffler, The Third Wave (New York: William Morrow, 1980).

16.  The Print Project, The Techno/Peasant Survival Manual (New York: Bantam Books, 1980).

17.  Louis Mertes, "Doing Over Your Office—Electronically," Harvard Business Review 59 (March/April 1981):127-35.

18.  Carl Rosenfeld and Scott Brown, "The Labor Force Status of Older Workers," Monthly Labor Review 102 (November 1979):12-18.

19.  Leon, "The Employment-Population Ratio."

# 3

# REDUCED WORK TIME AS
# A FAMILY POLICY ISSUE

> Home is the place where, when you have to go
> there, they have to take you in.
> I should have called it something you somehow
> haven't to deserve.
>
> Robert Frost

Those who have urged increased opportunities for job sharing
and permanent part-time work, particularly at the professional and
managerial level, have often done so on the grounds of equality of
opportunity for women. Women, it is argued, deserve the right to
compete on an equal basis with men with equivalent qualifications.
Yet women are doubly disadvantaged because of their gender. First
of all, only women can bear children, and childbearing may force
them to interrupt their careers at a critical time—at the time when
their age cohort is experiencing its most rapid career development.
Secondly, although child rearing can be, and often is, a shared
parental role, in reality most women carry the larger share of responsibility for both the family and the home. Employers, however,
tend to impose expectations on career employees, male or female,
that are based on a linear-separable concept of time. These expectations—long hours of work, frequent travel, and periodic
transfers, for example—seriously conflict with family duties. The
solution to this dilemma, some argue, is to allow women with these
role conflicts to work shorter work weeks.

This argument obviously has merit; but policies that seek to
achieve equity often have unintended consequences. Women who
are given special employment privileges because of their status as
wives and mothers may find themselves regarded in the organization

29

as separate and not necessarily equal; they may have less role strain but be no closer to equality. The differential treatment may perpetuate the stereotype that working women are dual-career wives, while working men are single-career husbands. Further, while fairness and equity are clearly laudable goals, as a practical matter organizations must weigh those goals not only against the goals of various constituencies within the organization but also against goals of efficiency.

Rather than arguing for reduced work-time opportunities on the basis of reducing institutional discrimination against women, it may be more fruitful to look at the origins of existing practices, the changes that are occurring in family roles for both women and men, and the impact of changing roles on organizations and on families. One should not, however, lose sight of the fact that the major impetus for change has been the enormous increase in women's labor force participation since the 1960s.

It is surely unnecessary to detail the social changes of recent years. Women of all ages, but particularly married women, even those with school-age and preschool children, are entering the labor market and remaining in the labor market at a rate never before experienced. The stereotype family of a generation ago, an employed husband (the breadwinner) with dependent wife and children, accounts for only a small proportion of contemporary households. It is necessary, however, to understand some of the changes that are taking place in family form. Young people are marrying at a slightly later age; they are postponing the age at which they bear the first child; and they are limiting the size of the family to one or two children. Cohabiting relationships are fairly common, but more commonly as a prelude to marriage rather than as a permanent lifestyle. Most young people plan eventually to marry and to have children.[1] Divorce rates are also higher than ever before, for families with or without children. Although most divorced people remarry, the high divorce rate contributes to the increased number of single-person households, single-parent families, and families that include a stepparent.

It is clear that while marriage is still the dominant form of lifestyle today, the form of married life has changed. Instead of one single family model, a pluralistic model exists. Because there is no longer one predominant family form, there is also no longer one predominant model of a job holder. The needs and expectations of contemporary job holders are as diverse, as pluralistic, as the number of family forms. A uniform set of compensation and career-development policies, devised for the stereotypical breadwinner, may represent less than the optimal form for a contemporary job holder, who may be a man or woman in a dual-career household—with or without children in residence, a man or woman in a single-career household—with or without dependent children in residence, a divorced or remarried man or woman, a woman or man with dependent nonresident children, or some combination of these.

This chapter will show that:

1. Employment and family policies that affect the distribution of income and benefits are based on an assumption of a family form that no longer predominates.

2. Although the rigid segregation of sex roles within the family has decreased, organizations tend to support a <u>masculine model of work</u> that assumes that segregation.

3. The masculine model of work creates stress and adversely affects families that differ from the traditional breadwinner model.

## "FAMILY POLICY" IN THE UNITED STATES

There is no uniform and explicit federal policy or body of policies that affects or regulates family life in this country, as there is in some Western countries; nor is it clear that there ought to be. The absence of such policy is often noted, and arguments can be offered for and against the creation of a family policy.[2] At this point, the probability that any comprehensive policy will emerge seems remote at best. Advocates of family policy seem unable to agree even on a definition of "family," which suggests a deep division on policy issues.

Nevertheless, there does exist a strong commitment to the concept of the family as the basic unit of the society, and there is a vast array of laws, programs, rules, and practices, both formal and informal, that implicitly and explicitly reflect that commitment. This collective policy, particularly those elements of it that affect the distribution of income, relies on a family model that describes less than 15 percent of all American households. When considering arguments for reduced work time, it is essential to look at the impact of that family model and at the relevance of shifting and emerging family models.

### The Breadwinner Model

Before the Industrial Revolution, the family was considered the basic unit of production; later it came to be considered the basic unit of consumption.[3] With that change came standardization of both work schedules and compensation.

Standard and uniform work schedules were first adopted because the rate of production was determined by industrial machinery. Heavy investment in machinery made it essential that the machines be kept in constant use; hence the introduction of shift work, with two 12-hour shifts per day. Over the years there has been a reduction in the hours of work, but the notion of a fixed schedule has persisted, even into the postindustrial society.

With the beginning of the labor movement and the rise of the scientific management movement in the early twentieth century, employers began to offer a standard pay rate. Since the overwhelming majority of employees were married men with dependent wives and families, wages had to be adequate to meet the needs of the breadwinner. As tax-free "fringe benefits" were added to the compensation plan, benefits were extended to the workers' dependents. Over the years, the collective bargaining system and a body of labor law have institutionalized protection for the job holder and his or her family against illness and loss of income. It is only recently that the assumption inherent in these policies, of the job holder as breadwinner, has begun to be challenged.

The Social Security system is a case in point. Introduced in the 1930s, it provides retirement and disability benefits to the worker, based on the history of indexed earnings on which the employee and the employer have paid payroll taxes. The dependent spouse of the worker may draw 50 percent of the worker's benefit. A wife who has worked under the Social Security system may draw either benefits on her own earnings or benefits as a wife, but she may not draw both. (The same situation exists for a husband, but the discussion here will consider the wife.) Often there is little difference, since her earnings are apt to be considerably lower than her husband's, and she is apt to have been in and out of the labor force over her lifetime. Whichever benefit she chooses to draw, the couple receives a lower return for its contributions than the couple where only one member has worked in covered employment.

Prior to 1979, a dependent wife's benefit was vested after 20 years of marriage. In 1979, the vesting period was reduced to ten years, but still the divorced or widowed wife is unable to combine her dependent's benefits with any that accrue from her own earnings, either before or after her marriage. In short, this very significant social program, despite recent changes, contains considerable vestiges of its original conception: social security for the breadwinner and his dependent wife. [4]

The provision of fringe benefits by employers also continues to reflect the presumption that the wage earner is a family's breadwinner. Employers increasingly serve as "mini-welfare organizations," [5] providing everything from pension to health-care costs and pay for time not worked. These benefits can represent up to 40 percent of the total payroll, even though they are still referred to as "fringe benefits." Typically, these benefit programs provide protection for the worker's family as well.

This mini-welfare system has come to be perceived as a right in modern organizations. At a minimum, full-time workers expect to receive health insurance, plus such pay-for-time-not-worked benefits as sick leave, holiday pay, and vacation pay. Ironically, many employers offer no benefits for part-time workers, regardless of the number of hours worked or the length of service. The full-time worker is presumed to be the breadwinner; the part-time worker is, presumably, someone's dependent.

The Pluralistic Model

This breadwinner stereotype, like most stereotypes, has a basis in reality—and, like most stereotypes, it is resistant to change, even when it no longer describes accurately the stereotyped group. Social and demographic changes in family life and family roles have been well documented in recent years, whether or not the causes of change have been fully explicated.

In the introduction to the third edition of their Family in Transition, family sociologists Arlene and Jerome Skolnick point out some of the demographic changes that have occurred in the decade since their first edition. Among those mentioned are:

1. The strong decline in the birth rate, which is now at its lowest point in American history.

2. The rapid rise in the divorce rate. Despite the fact that the rate has leveled off, it is still the highest in American history.

3. The increase in the number of unmarried couples living together, along with a change in attitude toward such arrangements. Living together without marrying is now relatively common not only among the young and the poor, but also among middle-class adults, especially among educated and professional persons.

4. The increase in the number of single-person households, which now account for one in every five households. This group consists of two subgroups: young people who have not yet married; and the formerly married, mostly older people who have lost a spouse.[6]

The most dramatic changes in life within the family have occurred because of the enormous increase in the labor-force participation of women. By 1978 nearly half of all married women were in the labor force, and predictions are that the proportion will increase to 55 percent by 1990.[7]

Among couples where the wife works full time, her earnings, on the average, account for 38 percent of the family's income. As a result, such a family on the average has a higher total income than a family in which there is a full-time homemaker, in spite of the loss of services of the homemaker and the additional costs incurred through having the wife work.

Women who work tend to marry at a later age and to have fewer children. Very few, however, forgo marriage or child rearing altogether.

According to the Skolniks:

> Ironically . . . many of the difficulties besetting family life today are the consequence of some very positive changes; the decline of infant mortality and death rates in general, the fact that people are living longer, the use of birth control, the spread of mass education, the increasing control of the individual over basic life decisions (whether to marry, when to marry, whom to marry, whether or not to have children, and how many to have).[8]

The result of holding on to a set of assumptions that is no longer viable is that, to a large extent, policies and practices may no longer meet the welfare needs of a majority of workers. Many couples with two full-time paychecks have redundant health insurance covering themselves and their children, whether or not they have children. A single mother may have no health-care insurance because she cannot find full-time work. A couple with two incomes may have extensive fringe benefits, high income (and high income taxes), and too little time.

Organizations are increasingly being faced with a changing set of expectations from employees in this pluralistic work force. Increasingly, emphasis is being put on the need for the employer to adapt to the changing requirements of employees, rather than the reverse—rather than the need for families to adapt to the inflexible norms of the organizations, both in terms of work and career patterns and in terms of pay and benefits.

## ORGANIZATIONS AND THE LOSS OF THE SINGLE-CAREER MALE

Like the breadwinner stereotype, a masculine, or patriarchial, model of work has long been the cornerstone of organizational career systems. This masculine model requires men to put their jobs first—before all other aspects of their lives, to work long hours, to travel, to transfer, to compete vigorously for power and position in the organization, and to respond to whatever prescriptions the organization imposes. As women have demanded access to career opportunities in organizations, they have been taught, trained, and prodded either to adopt the masculine model or to forgo the organization's rewards. Much of what is currently being offered as management training for women is no more than remedial management training, aimed at socializing women into accepting the male model of work.[9] As the number of married women pursuing careers has increased by enormous proportions in recent years, the challenge to the masculine model of work has come not only from these women, but from men as well; they too experience the conflicts that come with dual roles.

The masculine model of work is based on the presumption of a single-career couple with rigid segregation of roles. The increase in the number of dual-career couples is having a profound effect on the workplace as well as on the family. Evidence of the extent of the problem exists in the number of employees who are refusing to accept transfers, even when promotions depend on willingness to transfer. Estimates of the number of employees who are refusing range as high as 50 percent.[10] Refusing to transfer is, however, only the most overt and dramatic manifestation of a social change that is occurring in many less discernible ways.

The distinctions between dual-career and single-career couples can be demonstrated using an ideal-type methodology. For the sake of the discussion, "career" is used here to mean "those types of job sequences that require a high degree of commitment and that have a continuous developmental character."[11] For the moment at least, a distinction is being made between two-career and two-paycheck families. It will be clear, however, that many of the dysfunctions of current employment schedules apply to those forms, as well.

In order to make the contrast between dual-career and single-career couples, the ideal type will compare three sets of characteristics: the division of tasks and roles within the household, the integration or differentiation of job and leisure, and the priorities that prevail within the household.


Single-Career Couples

For the single-career couple, tasks and roles are divided along traditionally sex-related lines. The male is the provider, the breadwinner. His participation in home maintenance or family activities is confined to specific areas of activities and to specific times. Success, autonomy, and self-respect come to the male through his achievements on the job. His ability to earn determines the family's lifestyle and standard of living. His masculinity is involved in his ability to provide for and protect his family. The social status associated with his occupation or his position determines, to a very large extent, the family's social as well as its economic status.

Pressure to succeed is strong, so strong that it often leads to what Maccoby calls careerism—a constant anxiety not usually tied to any particular event or knowledge, but to loss of control:

> He is afraid that external events beyond his control
> or his inability to control himself will damage or
> destroy his career.[12]

The result of careerism for a majority of the executives in Maccoby's study was detachment from close relationships with associates, from family and friends, and from social responsibilities to the community.[13]

The female in the single-career couple fulfills the traditional roles of wife and mother. Hers is the responsibility for seeing that the home is well run and well ordered. Part of the role involves protecting the provider from household concerns that might produce stress and pressure and distract him from his career. Her femininity is attached to her success in this role. If she holds a paid job outside the home her earnings are secondary, supplementing the primary income, and often earmarked for specific expenses or luxuries. Her job always comes second to her responsibilities at home and is never allowed to inflict hardship on the family. Success for the woman in a single-career couple comes not from what she does but from what she is. Her status comes through his achievements.

Corporate wives have additional duties and responsibilities associated with the role of wife. These may include everything from emotional support to actual performance of corporate tasks that would otherwise be paid for.[14] They will almost surely include entertaining clients or colleagues in one's own home and participating in company-sponsored or job-related social activities. Her willingness and ability to perform well in this role are essential to his success. The single career is in fact a two-person career.[15]

For the single-career couple the distinction between what is job-related activity and what is leisure may be unclear at best. The advancement of the career may require membership in certain social, civic, religious, or professional organizations. The executive or his wife may feel compelled to play golf (or tennis, bridge, or poker) with other members of the firm or with clients. Participation in these informal activities may be essential to success in the organization. At the same time, frequent transfer or travel policies may result in patterns of propinquity in which a couple's genuine friends are drawn from among co-workers. Corporate wives differ a great deal in how they perceive and react to these expectations[16]—but whether or not they find them enjoyable, most agree that they are obligatory.

For the single-career couple, finally, the demands of the career will most frequently take priority over concerns of the family or of any other competitor for attention.[17] The family is dependent on the career both financially and socially, and hence is dependent on the organization. The family has a single and single-minded objective—the success of the provider; organizational requirements must come before all others. The literature on corporate wives abounds with examples: fathers who have never attended a child's birthday party, graduation, or school performance; families who have lived in a dozen different locations while children were growing up; women who have coped with enormous difficulties alone rather than disturb a harried executive at work; family vacations spoiled; a wife's career or profession aborted; cherished ideals and commitments relinquished to the demands of the career.[18]

Many organizations have developed a variety of programs aimed at socializing women into the role of corporate wife and reducing conflicts that may arise between career and family demands. Many wives, clearly, have found the rewards in this lifestyle well worth the sacrifices.

The purpose here is not to debate the relative merits of these two models but to describe the differences. In the single-career couple, success is defined in traditional terms: high-status position, high salary, material possessions. These symbols of success are clearly understood and are measurable; one's success or failure is apparent. The sacrifices required to attain success may be less readily measurable or apparent, but the priorities are clear and the pay-offs are valued.[19]

Dual-Career Couples

When describing an ideal type for the single-career couple, an abundance of evidence exists to suggest that the model closely matches reality. The phenomenon of the dual-career couple is less thoroughly documented; it is newer and still in the process of evolving. Thus, while the ideal type for the single-career couple is a descriptive model, the ideal type presented here for the dual-career couple is a normative one. Nevertheless, it is possible to describe such a couple, using the same characteristics that were used to describe the single-career couple: roles of husband and wife, differentiation between work and leisure, and priorities of career and family life. It is also possible to find evidence that this model is becoming increasingly prevalent.

In the ideal-type dual-career marriage, all roles and tasks are shared, rather than divided along traditional sex-role lines. The woman contributes a substantial share of the household income, sharing the provider or breadwinner role. She may earn less than her husband, but her income is essential to the family's standard of living, rather than a supplement earmarked for specific expenses. Further, it is understood that as her career develops her income will increase and may equal or exceed that of the male.

Just as the role of the provider is shared, so also is the role of nurturer shared. In this ideal-type dual-career marriage, decisions about who shall perform given tasks are made according to ability, convenience, or preferences, rather than according to the criterion of sex-appropriate roles. Even if the sharing of household tasks is not absolutely equal, at the very least the husband will assume more of the responsibility for his own personal needs. If there are children in this home, the man will share such responsibilities as picking up and delivering children at school or day care, attending school conferences or events, and staying at home when necessary with a sick child.

The role of corporate wife disappears in this model. Women who are pursuing careers are not available to carry out the duties of the corporate wife; men who are pursuing careers are also unavailable to play the role of corporate wife. For each individual, this clearly presents a hazard to career development. For the corporation it constitutes a loss of considerable resources that have been a part of the traditional two-person career. In the dual-career couple, neither spouse bears the full burden for providing the family's social status and standard of living; neither spouse achieves status vicariously through the achievements of the other.

The dual-career couple differentiates between career and leisure activities and spends considerably less of its nonjob time on the former. For the dual-career couple, time often becomes its most scarce and therefore most valued resource. The woman with a career may be unwilling to devote her discretionary time to entertaining or to recreation activities that will enhance her husband's career. The man who shares responsibility for home and family with a career woman may choose not to spend his scarce leisure time in job-related recreation, to enhance either her career or his own.[20] When time is the scarce resource, couples tend to find ways to maximize the utility of time that is available.[21]

In the dual-career couple there are conflicting priorities: between the two careers and between each career and the coupled relationship. Decisions cannot be made solely on the basis of what is best for one career; the effect on both careers and on the marriage must be considered. It may be in this area that the greatest role strain occurs; there are daily decisions to be made that may affect one or the other's career or the relationship itself. Long before a couple faces the problem of deciding whether one or the other should accept a promotion that requires a transfer, there may have been many decision points where priorities conflict. These may vary from a decision on which parent stays home from work with a sick child to deciding which spouse continues to work in his or her present job while the other attends graduate school.

It is also in this area that the greatest problem occurs for organizations that are based on the assumptions of the masculine model of work. They offer support for the single-career model and not for the dual-career model, and are unprepared to respond to the needs of the dual-career couple.[22] Certainly for management this new breed of couple poses some perplexing problems.

Mixed priorities may constitute a mixed blessing for the dual-career couple. On the one hand they may enjoy greater freedom, and on the other hand they may face increased constraints. When the provider role is shared, the couple's dependence on the organization is reduced. Members of a dual-career couple may experience less fear of economic or social disaster if the corporation is displeased. The consequences associated with refusal to be co-opted are considerably reduced. On the other hand, greatly prized opportunities for personal growth or for advancement may have to be bypassed. The costs to a career that occur when another career, and a commitment to another individual, are given equal weight in decision making are never direct and measurable, nor are the benefits of setting priorities in this way. For the single-career couple, success is clearly defined and measurable; one knows when one has achieved it. For the dual-career couple success tends to be defined in more intrinsic and personal ways, certainly in less measurable ways. Hence for the dual-career couple, both costs and benefits are more subjective than for the single-career couple.[23]

Table 1 summarizes the characteristics of the ideal-type single-career and dual-career couples.

TABLE 1

The Ideal-Type Couples

| Characteristics | Single-Career Couple | Dual-Career Couple |
|---|---|---|
| Division of tasks and roles | Tasks are rigidly divided according to appropriate sex role. | Tasks are divided according to ability, convenience, or preference. |
| | Husband is provider; wife is nurturer. | Roles are shared. |
| Job/leisure | Considerable integration of job and leisure exists. Many social or recreational activities are undertaken to advance career. | Differentiation of job and leisure exists. Leisure activities are freely chosen and pursued for their own sake, rather than prescribed by the organization. |
| Priorities | Career always has priority. Success is valued and is defined as high-status job, high income. | Priorities are divided among the two careers and the coupled relationship. Success is valued and is defined in terms of self-fulfillment. |

Source: Compiled by the author.

## FAMILIES AND THE LOSS OF THE SINGLE-CAREER WIFE

Long before the flower children of the 1960s were rejecting the oppressiveness of organizational life, writers as disparate as Lionel Tiger[24] and William H. Whyte[25] were warning of the human costs, not only to the executive but also to the family, of contemporary organizational life. The literature of the twentieth century abounds with fictional examples portraying the glory and horror of the lives of men who have relentlessly pursued the bitch goddess success, only to end up rich and lonely or, occasionally, poor and beloved. More recently, however, the inequities of the system for women seeking career opportunities have been addressed. Criticisms of the masculine model of work have resulted in two ways to address the problem: employers are encouraged either to make special concessions for women who need to fulfill two roles or to provide assistance to couples in coping with the expectations of the organization.

Increasingly, the literature is looking at the dysfunctions of the masculine model of work for all workers, including males, and also at the impact on family life when the wife and mother is a member of the full-time labor force. A number of issues are pertinent, among them the degree to which work and family life conflict; the significance of child care; the quality of life within the family; women's earnings and economic contribution; the contribution of household production; and the stresses created by affluence.

## Conflict between Work and Family

A significant minority of workers who live in families experience either moderate or severe conflict between their jobs and their family life.[26] Researchers at the University of Michigan's Survey Research Center have found that over one-third of the workers in the Quality of Employment Survey reported such conflict. The most common sources of conflict reported were "excessive work time," "schedule conflicts," and "fatigue and irritability."

As might be expected, working parents in the study reported conflict more often than did other workers, and parents of preschool-age children reported conflict more often than did parents of school-age children. Men were more likely to report "excessive work time" as a source of conflict; women were more likely to report "schedule conflicts" and "fatigue and irritability."

Contrary to expectations, however, employed women did not report work-family conflict significantly more often than did employed men. Whether the spouse was employed made little difference; even comparing employed husbands and employed wives did not produce significant differences. In short, conflict exists between work and family for at least one-third of the working population who live in families, and that conflict occurs on the average as often for men as it does for women.

## Child Care

One very significant effect of changing family forms is the increasing number of children whose mothers are now in the paid labor force and who, therefore, are receiving some form of group care or surrogate mothering. Since nurturing has traditionally been the area in which women's feminine role has been most universally expressed, the issue of the effect on children of the mother's employment is a highly controversial one and one that has been explored in depth.

The research literature is very nearly universal in finding that children who receive high-quality day care suffer no harmful effects.[27] The problem, of course, is that not all children receive high-quality day care. The problems and causes are complex, involving among other things the financial need for women to work and the low value attached to child care.

Human babies, unlike other mammals, have a very long period of physical dependency and helplessness after birth. They require constant protection and nurturing for several years. Responsibility for that care has always been assigned to the parents in the United States, in contrast to countries and societies where that care is perceived as a societal responsibility. In the single-career family, the responsibility has typically been delegated to the mother, who provided the service without pay. Norwegian sociologist Erick Grønseth reasons that this explains why those who provide the service are unable to receive adequate pay for it.[28]

Family in-home day care—in which a mother takes one or two youngsters into her own home to earn extra money or as company for her own children—has been and continues to be a major source of day care. Increasingly, however, mothers are in the paid labor force themselves and are purchasers of, rather than suppliers of, child care. Since women typically earn low wages, they have limited ability to pay for child care, and that further depresses the supply. Parents who earn high incomes can probably find good-quality surrogate mothering. Low-income families may receive child-care subsidies and may be eligible for publicly provided care. In between are the middle-income families for whom the income of both parents is essential, who must have reliable and responsible child care, and who have great difficulty in finding that care at an affordable price.

This is not to suggest that children of working parents are not getting adequate care or that they are being either abused or neglected. In fact, very little is known about either the type of day care or the quality of nurturing that these children are receiving.[29] It does seem reasonable to suggest that the difficulty in securing satisfactory child care puts a considerable strain on working parents. The child-care provider may impose schedule requirements that are as rigid as those imposed by the organization, leaving the child and the parents caught in a perpetual juggling act.

## The Family's Quality of Life

Whether or not the family includes children, the dual-career family lacks the luxury of the services of a "wife." Scott Burns has taken this familiar plaint of working couples to heart and has analyzed the household economy as a productive economy. He concludes that, unlike the market economy, the household economy is healthy, stable, and growing.[30] The household economy, according to Burns, consists of:

> the sum of the goods and services produced within all the households in the United States. This includes among other things, the value of shelter, home-cooked meals, all the weekend built patios and barbecues in suburban America, painting and wallpapering, home sewing, laundry, child care, home repairs, volunteer services to the community and to friends, the produce of the home garden, and the transportation services of the private automobile.[31]

Burns is going far beyond the frequent studies that attempt to impute to a housewife the economic value of her contribution to the family's well-being. He approximates the value of the household economy as "equal to the entire amount paid out in wages and salaries by every corporation in the United States" and puts the return on investment (in goods and services) at "almost equal to the net profits of every corporation in the United States."[32]

Clearly, when both members of a couple work at full-time jobs outside the home, the time available for household production decreases. Some of this lost production can be replaced in the market economy: meal planning and preparation, child care, housecleaning, and lawn care. Some of it will be forgone, however. Volunteer services to the community and to friends—activities like youth groups and school-parent organizations, for example—are already feeling the loss of the single-career wife. The greatest loss, however, may be in that portion of the household economy that is most labor-intensive, that is, personal services, including the care, feeding, and transportation of the family members.

## The Family's Economic Well-being

Consider a spouse who decides to seek full-time market work. (This discussion will consider the wife, but is equally applicable to the husband.) In such a case, a wife chooses to exchange time for dollars. She will forgo some household production, continue to perform some household tasks, and share others, particularly child care, with her spouse. The value of the additional income, however, is subject to some adjustments. Additional out-of-pocket expenses will be incurred, the largest amounts for transportation, clothing, and retirement deductions. [33]

Household production is not counted as part of the couple's income, so it can be regarded as nontaxable income. Market wages, on the other hand, are taxed. Furthermore, the second income is taxed not at the marginal tax rate for its own earnings level, but at the marginal tax rate that is achieved when the two salaries are added together. [34] In other words, the couple must pay a "marriage penalty."

In sum, the woman who chooses to remain out of the paid labor force produces goods and services that are recognized neither by the society nor by the family as part of the family's income. When she enters the paid labor force she and the family, as well as the larger society, will forgo the benefits of that production, much of which is labor-intensive service activity. She will increase her family's income, but will incur additional work-related expenses. Further, her family tax obligation will be the same as that of a single-career couple with the same income but that also enjoys the productivity of a full-time homemaker.

The issue here is not whether women are better off, or their families are better off, if they stay out of the labor force. The majority of working families could not survive with a single paycheck, even if either spouse preferred not to work. Also, a great many women will continue to work outside the home even in the absence of a financial necessity. The important issue is that, given a masculine model of work, women and men are given what Constantina Safilios-Rothschild has called an "all or nothing" choice. [35] They must work full time and continuously throughout their lives or forgo much of the security and many of the benefits that come with labor-market participation. When they work full time, though, the family not only forgoes the opportunity for household production, but also incurs increased earnings expenses and higher taxes.


## Affluence, Consumption, and Stress

John Kenneth Galbraith asserts that:

It is a prime tenet of modern economic belief—one that is central to the established economics and powerfully

reinforced by advertising and salesmanship—that happiness is a function of the supply of goods and services
consumed.[36]

If that were true, then surely the two-earner family would
enjoy its increased affluence. The modern household has available
a virtual wonderland of labor-saving and time-saving artifacts that
can be purchased with the additional income from a wife's market
earnings. Technology has provided the basic accouterments of
modern civilized existence—running water, electricity, central
heat, refrigeration. These basics, combined with the semiconductor, make possible mind-boggling conveniences—programmable
electronic devices that cook, clean, and sew. It sometimes appears
that we have at last reached that utopian age only dreamed of by
Aristotle:

> There is only one condition on which we can imagine
> managers not needing subordinates, and masters not
> needing slaves. This condition would be that each
> [inanimate] instrument could do its own work, at the
> word of command or by intelligent anticipation. . . .
> As a shuttle should weave of itself, and a plectrum
> should do its own harp playing.[37]

If the electronic age is making workers obsolete, creating unemployment in the market place, is it also making housework obsolete,
creating unemployment in the household economy? Isn't the contemporary family able to use its new affluence to increase its
leisure enjoyment?

Apparently not! The evidence shows that the time spent in
housework has not, in fact, changed materially over the last 50
years for women not in the paid labor force.[38] One reason, according to Galbraith, is that technology has reduced the amount of
physical strength necessary to maintain the household, but at the
same time a number of social and economic forces have raised the
standards of performance. Ever larger houses and gardens require ever increasing amounts of upkeep and maintenance; city
living reduces the necessity of producing goods oneself but increases
the time required to purchase them. City children require considerably closer supervision than do rural youngsters. Rather than
freeing us from arduous labor, the increasing acquisition of goods
increases our drudgery. We can enjoy the luxuries only if we can
delegate the labor. Unlike the masters of Aristotle's time, though,
the contemporary household has no servants, much less slaves,
and the lack of servants to whom one can delegate the labor puts a
constraint on consumption. The higher the family's income, the

greater the volume and complexity of consumption, and the greater
the number of tasks required.

Given that limitation, time, rather than money, becomes the
scarce resource. Steffan B. Linder, in his seminal work, The
Harried Leisure Class,[39] points out that affluence and scarcity are
relative terms, and that economic growth produces only partial
affluence. Increasing affluence provides access to more goods but
not to more services. Services require time, and the availability
of time is limited. It cannot literally be stored or saved. Total
affluence, then, is a logical fallacy. Increasing affluence, because
it is only partial, has brought not increasing tranquility but an increasingly hectic pace—we have more and more goods, which require time, but no more time. Linder's rather gloomy prediction
is that we will see in the future an increasingly hectic tempo, an
expanding mass of goods requiring maintenance time, and increasing hardship for those in need of services.

"Partial affluence" clearly describes the situation of the dual-
career couple. Two paychecks, even taxed at the combined rate for
both of them, may provide more than enough dollars to meet the
family's consumption demands. Two full-time jobs may severely
restrict the amount of time available for consumption, for maintenance, or for leisure.

## IMPLICATIONS

That social and organizational support for the masculine
model of work persists is well documented.[40] Also well documented
is the fact that this pattern is not only discriminatory to women,
but dysfunctional to men, to the family, to the organization, and
ultimately to the society.[41] Nevertheless, much of the current
literature is concerned with helping the dual-career couple cope
with the stresses created by the single-career work pattern, rather
than with a serious attempt to encourage organizations to adapt to
changing social patterns. As long as the problem remains a small
one for organizations and is seen primarily as a women's problem,
that approach is viable. If, however, as appears more and more to
be true, increasing numbers of men, the mainstream and the main
resources of the labor force, are experiencing conflict between work
and family life, then there is a need to re-examine policies and
practices.

Defenders of the masculine model of work will argue that employers invest significant amounts of training in professional and
managerial employees (thus incurring significant costs), that an
important aspect of the training is exposure to many facets and areas

of the organization's domain, and that the masculine model of work (the single-career model) provides the optimal training opportunities. Also, high training costs are more rapidly returned when an employee works full-time or more. According to this argument, the benefit/cost ratio for training is reduced when the employee opts for a reduced work schedule or a less aggressive career path.

Critics of the masculine model of work argue that the purpose of intensive exposure is indoctrination, not training. The purpose is to separate employees from everything in life that has meaning for them, so that ultimately they have no allegiance to anything but the organization.[42] Recruits undergo the equivalent of a corporate boot camp. Once socialized, the employees have internalized the goals and values of the organization. Each one comes to believe that "what's good for the company is good for me"; each becomes a modern-day chauvinist: my company, may it always be right, but right or wrong, my company!

Surely the time has come to examine the myriad policies and programs that affect employees, to identify those that are based on an assumption of a traditional family and a linear-separable concept of time, and to begin to revise old policies and adopt new ones that reflect the realities of an age when no single model of family life is adequate. It's time for pluralistic employment policies to meet the needs of a pluralistic society.

## NOTES

1. Mary Jo Bane, "Here to Stay: Parents and Children," in Family in Transition, ed. Arlene Skolnick and Jerome Skolnick, 3d ed. (Boston: Little, Brown, 1980).

2. Sheila Kamerman and Alfred Kahn, eds., Family Policy: Government and Families in Fourteen Countries (New York: Columbia University Press, 1978); cf. Rosabeth Moss Kanter, Work and Family in the United States: A Critical Review and Agenda for Research and Policy (New York: The Russell Sage Foundation, 1977).

3. Michael Young and Peter Willmott, The Symmetrical Family (New York: Pantheon Books, 1973).

4. Nancy M. Gordon, "Institutional Responses: The Social Security System," in The Subtle Revolution: Women at Work, ed. Ralph E. Smith (Washington, D.C.: The Urban Institute, 1979).

5. Robert J. Samuelson, "A Rebel with Cause," National Journal, April 26, 1980.

6. Skolnick and Skolnick, Family in Transition.

7. Ralph E. Smith, "The Movement of Women into the Labor Force," in The Subtle Revolution: Women at Work, ed. Ralph E. Smith (Washington, D.C.: The Urban Institute, 1979).

8. Skolnick and Skolnick, Family in Transition, p. 15.

9. See, for example, Betty Lehan Harragan, Games Your Mother Never Taught You (New York: Rawson Associates, 1977).

10. Cathleen Maynard, "Mobility and the Dual-Career Family," Personnel Journal (July 1979):468-82; cf. J. H. Foegen, "If it Means Moving, Forget it," Personnel Journal (August 1977): 414-16.

11. Rhona Rappaport and Robert Rappaport, Dual-Career Families Re-examined (London: Harper & Row, 1976), p. 9.

12. Michael Maccoby, The Gamesman: The New Corporate Leaders (New York: Simon and Schuster, 1976), p. 191.

13. Ibid.

14. Rosabeth Moss Kanter, Men and Women of the Corporation (New York: Basic Books, 1977), pp. 110-11; cf. J. M. and R. E. Pahl, Managers and Their Wives: A Study of Career and Family Relationships in the Middle Class (London: Allen Lane and the Penguin Press, 1971).

15. Ibid.

16. Ibid.; cf. Diane Margolis, The Managers: Corporate Life in America (New York: William Morrow, 1979).

17. Maccoby, The Gamesman, pp. 116-18.

18. Margolis, The Managers; cf. Lionel Tiger, "Is This Trip Really Necessary?" Fortune, September 1974, pp. 130-41, 182; William H. Whyte, "The Wives of Management," Fortune, October/November, 1951.

19. Daniel Yankelovich, "Work, Values, and the New Breed," in Work in America: The Decade Ahead, ed. Jerome Rosow and Clark Kerr (New York: D. Van Nostrand, 1979), p. 11.

20. Barrie S. Greiff, M.D., and Preston K. Munter, M.D., Tradeoffs: Executive, Family and Organizational Life (New York: The New American Library, 1980).

21. John Menefee, "The Economics of Leisure: The Evolution of the Leisure-Labor Trade-Off in Economic Doctrines" (Ph.D. diss., Duke University, Department of Economics, 1974).

22. Rosen Benson and Thomas Jerdee, "Dual-Career Marital Adjustment: Potential Effects of Discriminatory Managerial Attitudes," Journal of Marriage and the Family (August 1975):565-72.

23. Yankelovich, "Work, Values, and the New Breed."

24. Tiger, "Is This Trip Really Necessary?"

25. Whyte, "The Wives of Management."

26. Joseph H. Pleck, Graham L. Staines, and Linda Lang, "Conflicts Between Work and Family Life," Monthly Labor Review 103 (March 1980):29-31.

27. Kristin A. Moore and Sandra L. Hofferth, "Women and Their Children," in The Subtle Revolution: Women at Work, ed. Ralph E. Smith (Washington, D.C.: The Urban Institute, 1979); cf. Kristin A. Moore and Isabell Sawhill, "Implications of Women's Employment for Home and Family Life," in Women Working: Theory and Facts in Perspective, ed. Ann Stromberg and Shirley Harkess (Palo Alto, Calif.: Mayfield, 1978).

28. Erick Grønseth, "The Breadwinner Trap," in The Future of the Family, ed. Louise Kapp Howe (New York: Simon and Schuster, 1972).

29. Kristin A. Moore and Sandra L. Hofferth, "Women and Their Children"; cf. Mary Jo Bane et al., "Child Care Arrangements of Working Parents," Monthly Labor Review 102 (October 1979): 50-56.

30. Scott Burns, Home Inc. (New York: Doubleday, 1975).

31. Ibid., p. 5.

32. Ibid., p. 6.

33. Clair Vickery, "Women's Economic Contribution to the Family," in The Subtle Revolution: Women at Work, ed. Ralph E. Smith (Washington, D.C.: The Urban Institute, 1979).

34. Gordon, "Institutional Responses."

35. Constantina Safilios-Rothschild, "Women and Work: Policy Implications and Prospects for the Future," in Women Working: Theories and Facts in Perspective, ed. Ann Stromberg and Shirley Harkess (Palo Alto, Calif.: Mayfield, 1978).

36. John Kenneth Galbraith, Economics and the Public Purpose (Boston: Houghton Mifflin, 1973).

37. Aristotle, The Politics of Aristotle, trans. and ed. Ernest Barker, (London: Oxford University Press, 1976).

38. JoAnn Vanek, "Time Spent in Housework," in The Economics of Women and Work, ed. Alice H. Amsden (New York: St. Martin's Press, 1980).

39. Steffan B. Linder, The Harried Leisure Class (New York: Columbia University Press, 1970).

40. Rosen Benson and Thomas Jerdee, "Sex Stereotyping in the Executive Suite," Harvard Business Review 52 (March/April 1974):45-58; cf. Marta Mooney, "Does it Matter if His Wife Works?" Personnel Administration, January 1981, pp. 43-49.

41. Grønseth, "The Breadwinner Trap"; cf. Kanter, Men and Women of the Corporation; Margolis, The Managers; Tiger, "Is This Trip Really Necessary?"; Pahl and Pahl, "Managers and Their Wives"; Whyte, "The Wives of Management"; Maccoby, "The Gamesman."

42. Margolis, The Managers.

# 4

## REDUCED WORK TIME AND
## ORGANIZATIONAL THEORY

The moral flabbiness of the exclusive worship of the
bitch-goddess success. That—with the squalid cash
interpretation put on the word success—is our national defense.

William James

Organizational theory has long been concerned with the problem of dealing concurrently with the utilitarian goals of organizations and the goals, both instrumental and expressive, of individuals.
The Hawthorne studies in the late 1920s raised questions about the
validity of the rational-economic model of human beings. In those
studies it became clear that social norms affected behavior in here-
tofore unconsidered and unexplained ways and that the relationship
between performance and rewards was a complex one indeed. Theorists since that time have sought adequate models to describe, explain, predict, and control the drives and needs that affect individual
behavior and that lead to maximum productivity.

Although extant theory is far from conclusive, certain premises have become a part of the conventional wisdom. It is generally
unquestioned that needs and drives can be divided loosely into two
categories: instrumental needs for salary and fringe benefits to
provide for the basic physiological needs of the worker and his or
her dependents; and expressive needs for meaning, identity, and
self-worth. Further, there is general agreement with the premise
that an employee will produce more when he or she perceives that
doing so will maximize either the extrinsic or the intrinsic rewards
associated with the job. These premises lead syllogistically to the
conclusion that when the organization offers both intrinsic and ex-

trinsic rewards for high productivity, then both the organization and the individual will maximize their goals.

Theory then turns to the problem of achieving the desired integration of individual and organizational goals. It should be absolutely clear to any observer, however, that the ulterior goal in all this is the organization's effectiveness. Certainly, however altruistic its motives, the underlying goal of an organization attempting to turn theory into practice is the maximization of its own utilitarian goals, rather than the self-actualization of members.

In recent years a variety of methods have been applied to the problem of integrating organizational and individual goals. These go under a variety of names, including Sociotech, Organizational Development, and Quality of Working Life. Although they vary considerably in technique, they have in common a belief in the efficacy of improving simultaneously productivity and job satisfaction.

These approaches, however, are based on assumptions that are questionable at best. First, they assume that all workers have internalized the masculine model of work and are imbued with the tenets of the traditional Protestant work ethic; second, they assume that organizations can, in general, be structured so that jobs can meet employees' expressive needs; and third, they assume that organizations can simultaneously maximize disparate and sometimes conflicting goals.

This chapter presents evidence that suggests that the traditional work ethic is undergoing some substantial changes and that a "leisure ethic" is emerging. Also, it argues that productivity is the appropriate domain of organizational theory, that organizations should limit themselves to adequately providing those extrinsic rewards that motivate performance and meet the instrumental needs of the employee, and that expressive needs and intrinsic rewards can best be met in leisure.


THE WORK ETHIC IN TRANSITION

The Origins of the Work Ethic

Historically, labor has been considered onerous at worst, an unpleasant duty at best. The early Greeks and Romans saw physical labor as the revenge of the gods on mankind, as altogether lacking in inherent value and dignity. The early Hebrews held a similar view, but they found that labor was necessary to expiate original sin. Early rabbinical literature, however, exalted human manual labor as a means of co-operating with God towards human salvation. The early Christians added a positive function: one could not only earn his own living but could also produce a surplus to share with the poor. Nevertheless, labor, in this view, had no intrinsic value, and wealth was to be despised.

Early Catholicism, specifically St. Augustine and St. Benedict, began to add new value and dignity to labor, albeit only as an instrument of expiation, purification, and charity. A hierarchy of values emerged that put manual labor at the lowest level, intellectual or creative activity in the middle, and prayer and contemplation at the apex.

As the Reformation approached and the church became more worldly, this view began to soften, but at no time was labor valued as an end in itself, for its own sake. It was valued only as a means of achieving the true end—the life hereafter.

It was Protestantism, as articulated by Martin Luther, that began to dignify labor by making any work a form of service to God. Duty was to labor, although not to profit, and to do the best job possible, no matter what the activity. All labor was seen as being equal before the Lord, hence all labor had the same dignity. One was to do one's best at any job; one was not to strive for better, higher-status work. [1]

John Calvin, more dour than any of the "dour Scots," added the requirement that man must work hard at all times, eschew pleasure, strive to get ahead, and accumulate his wealth. Labor was seen as a vocation. Our legacy from Calvin is that the religious fervor has abated but the value of labor and accumulated capital has persisted. [2]

Max Weber and others have asserted that modern capitalism, science and technology, and the concept of the division of labor all have their roots in Calvinism. [3] R. H. Tawney, on the other hand, argues that the Reformation itself was a response to social needs, that while puritanism helped to mold the social order, it was also molded by it. [4] For our purposes, the cause-and-effect relationships are less important than the recognition and understanding of the depth of the relationship between labor and religion.

With the coming of the Industrial Revolution, which was based on the concept of the division of labor and accompanied by the gradual loss of the view of work as a vocation serving God, nineteenth-century philosophers and sociologists became concerned with the prospect of work alienation. Karl Marx responded to Adam Smith, who saw the division of labor as beneficial to all workers, by warning that the necessary relationship between division of labor and the exchange economy reduced labor to a commodity and hence dehumanized all labor. According to Marx, workers become slaves, alienated not only from other individuals, but also from themselves. Labor provides the means for physical existence; only by not labor-

ing can workers express their individuality.[5] In this argument
Marx does not challenge the assumption that one is defined by one's
job and that one's job is central to one's life.

Another nineteenth-century sociologist, Emile Durkheim,
also expressed concern for the effects of the division of labor.
Durkheim predicted that the character of society would change from
one of "mechanical solidarity," where there is little room for individuality, to one of "organic solidarity," where there is an absence
of norms. In the latter state, there is a danger of anomie, a state
of rootlessness, normlessness, and alienation.[6]

Whether these early thinkers were accurate in their predictions of the effect of industrialization is a question frequently raised
and hotly debated. Data concerning job satisfaction and work-force
discontent are ambiguous and equivocal. Some portion of the work
force is discontented, but the extent and source of the discontent
are not fully understood; nor is the issue of whether the percentage
of discontented workers is static or growing.[7]

The Work Ethic Today

Changes are occurring in the society that deeply affect the relationship between workers and their organizations. To understand
those changes, it may be helpful to look at the "work ethic" as it
existed in the mid 1960s. A survey of basic American life values
undertaken by Daniel Yankelovich Inc. found that the majority of the
adult population at that time associated four cultural themes with
"work" (that is, with "job"):[8]

1. The "good provider" theme—being the "breadwinner"
means being a real man. Providing for one's own is linked to
masculinity.

2. The "independence" theme—work equals autonomy. Working means standing on one's own two feet and avoiding dependence on
others.

3. The "success" theme—hard work pays off and leads to success, usually in the form of owning one's own home, enjoying an
ever rising standard of living, and achieving a solid position in one's
community.

4. The "self-respect" theme—hard work of any kind has dignity. To work hard and to do one's best provide a feeling of self-
worth.

Ten years later, in the mid 1970s, Yankelovich's monitoring
of American life values revealed five cultural trends that, he asserts,

have deep significance for the meaning of success in the United States: reduced fears of economic insecurity, a weakening of the rigid division of tasks between the sexes, an increasing "psychology of entitlement" that is leading to the creation of new social rights, and spreading disillusionment with the cult of efficiency.

The old components of success—money, job status, posessions, and upward mobility for one's children—still count, but many people are beginning to believe that there is such a thing as enough money, particularly when earning more money entails sacrifices in terms of lifestyle. New ideas about success tend to revolve around various forms of self-fulfillment. The money, possessions, and occupational status that are the traditional symbols of success become means to self-realization and the fulfillment of one's potential, rather than ends in and of themselves.

Economic security continues to be dominant in people's lives, but today most people take it for granted. One consequence of this reduced fear of economic insecurity has been a lessening of the fear and guilt associated with a lessening of role rigidity in marriage. As Chapter 3 detailed, women are rapidly taking on a stronger economic role, working both for income and for self-fulfillment. As these changing roles for women are becoming more widely accepted, so also is the increased participation of men in daily household activities.

The "psychology of entitlement" refers to the psychological process by which one's wants or desires are converted into a set of presumed rights. In this process, "I want . . ." becomes translated into "I have a right to. . . ." While this process is far from new, it has accelerated in recent years and has been expressed in various social movements that have made themselves keenly felt. These include the women's movement, the gay rights movement, and the consumer movement.

Finally, Yankelovich finds an increasing rejection of the process of "rationalization" by which institutions and organizations strive to realize the ideals of cost effectiveness, division of effort, efficiency, measurement of results, and objectification of function. He finds that the counter culture's concern for the effect of overemphasis on efficiency, quantitative methods, and cost effectiveness has begun to spread to the general population. While the form it assumes is not nearly so doctrinaire as in the counter culture, there does seem to be a concern that too great an emphasis on efficiency and rationalization may be depriving us of some of the richness of life. [9]

Yankelovich's survey data have been supported and extended by Rosabeth Moss Kanter, who uses trend data analysis to identify changes occurring in work. [10] Kanter's research has identified five

significant trends: a large-increase in women's labor-force participation; a shift toward a younger, more educated labor force;
increasing fringe benefits and government attention to working conditions, especially health implications and schedules; a slightly
shifting position of organized labor, especially the growth in white-
collar unions; and equivocal and controversial data on job satisfaction and on whether work-force discontent has increased or remained at a steady, low level.

The following table presents a comparison of the cultural
trends identified by Yankelovich and Kanter:

| Yankelovich | Kanter |
|---|---|
| A change in the meaning of success | A shift toward a younger, more educated work force |
| Disillusionment with the "cult of efficiency" | Increase in the labor-force participation of women, par- |
| Weakening of the rigid division of tasks between the sexes | ticularly married women |
| Reduced fear of economic insecurity | Increased fringe benefits and government attention to work conditions |
| Increase in the "psychology of entitlement" | Slight shift in the position of organized labor; white-collar unions emphasizing work op- tions and labor-management committees |
| | Conflicting data on work-force discontent |

Kanter finds two new themes emerging. One, cultural and
expressive, reflects the concern that jobs should be a source of
self-respect and nonmaterial reward—challenge, growth, personal
fulfillment, interesting and meaningful work, the opportunity to ad-
vance in one's career and to accumulate wealth, and the chance to
lead a safe and healthy life. The other, a political theme, suggests
a concern for individual rights and power, for a further extension
of principles of equity and justice in the workplace. [11]

These emerging themes, in turn, affect the four themes identified by Yankelovich in his studies during the mid 1960s. The "independence" theme is growing stronger and is being internalized by
women as well as men. The "good provider" theme is undergoing
change as sex-linked roles in marriage become increasingly flexible,
especially among college-educated young people. The "self-respect"

theme—that any task, however menial, possesses inherent dignity if it is honest labor—will probably undergo rapid change. Dignity will be inherent in tasks that the individual calls "meaningful," according to whatever definition of that term the individual adopts. As self-fulfillment continues to usurp material goods and occupational status as a symbol of success, occupational-status hierarchies will continue to break down.

The "success" theme—the belief that hard work always pays off—will undergo the greatest change of all the themes, as the perception of an appropriate pay-off continues to change. In the past the pay-off for hard work came in the form of extrinsic rewards; in the future there will be far more emphasis on the quality of life and on intrinsic rewards of self-fulfillment as the appropriate pay-off.[12]

These findings clearly indicate that jobs continue to have both an expressive and an instrumental meaning for workers: an expressive meaning in terms of challenge and personal fulfillment and an instrumental meaning for income and income protection. The irony is that while these trends are becoming manifest, there is also evidence (discussed in Chapter 2) that jobs are increasingly becoming more routinized, more bureaucratic, more monotonous.[13]

At the same time, the debate on the nature and the extent of worker discontent extends to concern over declining productivity of workers, as reflected in the quantity, quality, and value of the tasks performed. Organizational literature contains extensive theoretical and empirical material that attempts to address these issues concurrently, that is, to devise methods of improving productivity by improving the quality of working life. The underlying assumptions of these efforts are that many jobs can be made intrinsically rewarding, that they will then meet the expressive expectations of the job holders, and that the job holders will then become more productive. The presumption is that there will be a mutually and equitably rewarding improvement.

However, these assumptions contain certain fallacies, which may account for the mixed results of organizational interventions. For example:

1. Little if any distinction is made between work and labor. All job tasks are considered to be at least potentially meaningful. "Work" is defined as any paid activity. Inadequate attention is paid to the distinction between jobs that involve "work" and those that involve only "labor."

2. These assumptions fail to recognize the distinctions between leisure, nonwork, free time, and idleness. At the same time they fail to recognize the relationship between work, as distinct from labor, and leisure.

3. These assumptions concentrate only on the individual's role as <u>job holder</u> and exclude from consideration any off-the-job existence. Hence, they assume that an individual's expressive needs for independence, success, and self-respect, as well as instrumental needs for money and security, can be met only on the job.

4. It is assumed that organizations can and should serve multiple purposes; in other words, that management can work to achieve the goals of the organization while providing opportunities for individual members to achieve their personal goals.

Before looking at the implications of the changing work ethic for organizational theory, one must consider as well the emerging leisure ethic.

AN EMERGING LEISURE ETHIC

The Origins of the Leisure Ethic

The early Greeks despised labor and those who labored; they prized leisure. Aristotle, in the <u>Politics</u>, describes leisure as "freedom from the necessity to labor."[14] Leisure was seen as a condition, characterized by the performance of activities carried on for their own sake, providing intrinsic pleasure and intrinsic happiness. It was an end in itself, not a means to an end, as preparation for labor would be; nor was it compensation for labor. Only two activities were considered worthy of the name leisure: music and contemplation. Leisure was synonymous with the good life; the polis existed to provide leisure, and only those who had attained leisure—freedom from the necessity to labor—were members of the polis.

Roman views of leisure were derived from the works of Plato, Aristotle, and Epicurus, and in turn influenced early Christian thought. "Contemplation" became seeking of religious truth, a search for God; "work" was what one did in one's free time. For St. Thomas and the early Catholics, work was only to provide necessities; the highest order of work was contemplation and prayer.[15]

This influence of Greek and Roman thought can be seen through the Middle Ages and the Renaissance, with its enormous concern for arts and letters. The development of music, poetry, art, mathematics, and philosophy was part of an expanded version of Aristotle's view of leisure as music and contemplation. As we saw earlier, it was the coming of the Reformation that elevated labor to an exalted position and reduced leisure to a concept of free time and idleness.

That men and women should have sought, much less won, a universal right to labor would have been unthinkable to Aristotle.

Contemporary definitions of leisure are numerous, overlapping, and often vague. Kelley has looked at the definitions of leisure and of nonwork used by leisure theorists since the early Greek days and has produced a paradigm using two dimensions: "discretion"—whether leisure is freely chosen or determined by job constraints or social pressure, and "work-relation"—whether leisure is independent of one's job or dependent on the meaning given to it by one's job.[16] The work-relation dimension includes not only the economic reward for tasks performed, but also the preparation, appearance, and other conforming behaviors required or rewarded by the job. The paradigm appears in Table 1.

TABLE 1

A Simplified Paradigm of Work and Leisure

| Work-relation | Discretion | |
| --- | --- | --- |
| | Chosen | Determined |
| Independent | Unconditional leisure | Complementary leisure |
| Dependent | Co-ordinated leisure | Preparation and recuperation |

Source: John R. Kelley, "Work and Leisure: A Simplified Paradigm," Journal of Leisure Research 4 (Winter 1972):50-61.

Unconditional leisure includes leisure that is undertaken primarily for its own sake, as an end in itself. The activity is chosen from among alternatives, not for its recuperative effects, not because it enhances the individual as a job holder, but only because of the pure joy of it.

Co-ordinated leisure is freely chosen and yet related to the job, co-ordinated with but not required by the job. An example would be the time a professor spends reading a scholarly journal, because it interests her, not because she is preparing a lecture or writing a paper.

Complementary leisure includes activities that are complementary to the job, independent of the work-relation but associated with occupational role-status expectations. Such an activity is not freely chosen but is determined to a significant degree by role expectations or by the need to compensate for work conditions. An example is the weekend golf a businessman plays with his boss or with clients. The distinction between unconditional and complementary leisure lies in the reasons that a given activity was chosen; the crucial distinction lies in the worker's perception of freedom not to participate or in the alternatives available.

"Preparation and recuperation" refers to nonjob activities that are "socially determined and related to work in form and content," either preparation for work or recuperation. The distinction, again, is choice. Activities in this area would be those that the job holder was required to undertake as a condition of further employment or that the job holder felt compelled to carry out because fatigue from the job left no other perceived choices.[17]

In common usage, activities in any of the four designations are considered nonwork, and unconditional, co-ordinated, and complementary leisure are all considered leisure. Leisure theorists agree that unconditional leisure is leisure; they might consider either co-ordinated or complementary leisure to be leisure.

Economic theory, too, has failed to distinguish between leisure and "free time" and, as a result, has relegated leisure to a secondary role as an economic variable. John Menefee examined the models of leisure used by the Neoclassical School, Marx, Veblen, the Chicago School, and the London School of Economics. He found that each considered leisure as the residual of work, as activities where time savings were ignored.[18] He argues that leisure is an activity that provides

> net positive utility of time expenditure for the individual. It may be income or nonincome generating work or play. Moreover, it is an activity that is produced and/or consumed voluntarily, subject to the appropriate efficiency conditions. It is an activity in which there is no sense of alienation of purpose or being.[19]

Leisure activities are based on some form of efficiency or maximization criteria. Individuals allocate their resources, especially their time, to make optimal use of the resources in the production and consumption of leisure activities. Leisure is no longer viewed as the antithesis of work—there are no specific criteria to differentiate between work and leisure; leisure may include the set of activities by which one earns one's living.[20]

At this point, it would be hard to disagree with John Neulinger's statement that "the term leisure is very like the term intelligence; everybody uses it but hardly anyone can agree on what
it means. "[21] What is important for the purposes of this discussion
is a concept of leisure, rather than a precise definition. The concept would characterize leisure as activities undertaken freely,
chosen from among alternatives, and pursued for the personal
pleasure and satisfaction that they provide. It would exclude activities that are undertaken because they are prescribed by the job
or role and activities that are perceived as necessary to compensate for or recover from job requirements. It would include activities for which the individual also receives pay. It would recognize
that individuals allocate their resources, particularly their time,
to maximize the utility of their leisure activities. It would recognize the distinction between "job" and "work" and the relationship
between "work" and "leisure. " With this conception of leisure, it
becomes apparent that the expressive expectations of work that
Yankelovich reports may be satisfied in leisure activities, rather
than on the job.

A New Leisure Ethic

Leisure research has tended to concentrate on leisure activities and on time and money budgets. There has been, unfortunately, little systematic work on leisure attitudes. Neulinger and
Miranda Breit have developed a leisure attitude questionnaire that
identifies five dimensions of leisure attitudes: self–definition
through leisure of work, affinity for leisure, society's role in leisure planning, amount of perceived leisure, and amount of work or
vacation desired. This instrument has been widely used but in relatively small studies. [22]

The Central Life Interest instrument developed by Robert
Dubin in the mid 1950s has also been widely used. [23] The instrument measures "the choice of behavioral setting in which the individual prefers to act out a specified set of behaviors . . . whether
the respondent is work or nonwork oriented with respect to his preferred locale for behaving. " The early research on industrial workers indicated that, for three out of four, the job and the workplace
were not the central life interest. More surprising was the finding
that only 10 percent of the workers perceived their primary social
relationships as taking place on the job. The results suggest that
the individual's attachment to an employer is to the formal organization or to the technological aspects of the job. [24]

When Dubin and Daniel Goldman used the Central Life Interest instrument to study attitudes of middle managers, they found
that a majority had central life interests that were not in their jobs.
Their results suggest that middle managers and specialists can respond to the organization's "mandatory requirement for participation" without making the institution central to their lives. [25]
They conclude that:

1. Sources of attachment to work organizations focus on
characteristics of the formal organization and on the technical fea-
tures of the work.
2. People may become attached to an environment without
having it become central in their lives.
3. Attachment through formal and technological behavior
systems may be sufficient to produce effective performance; that
is, extrinsic rewards, sometimes called hygiene factors, may, in
fact, be sufficient motivators.
4. Efforts to improve quality of work settings so that they
become preferred areas for informal relations and self-actualization may be counterproductive.

> The effective detachment of man from work could be
> highly functional to their total life as citizens, rep-
> resenting progress toward a social system in which
> man's capacities, enjoyments, rewards and interests,
> for the first time in history, will be focused on non-
> productive activities. [26]

Dubin and Goldman fall into the semantic difficulties suggested
above; they apparently consider work and job to be the same and
look on nonjob activities as nonproductive. Nevertheless, their research and their conclusions support the notion that a new leisure
ethic is emerging.

Despite the lack of national survey data, there is evidence that
this emerging leisure ethic is sorely needed. Such an ethic would
have to be viewed as normative at this point, although there is clearly a good deal of evidence that it exists but has yet to be clearly articulated. Neulinger has described this new leisure ethic:

> The belief that the job can provide the basis for self-
> definition is simply no longer appropriate for millions
> and millions of people. A radical change in the belief
> of what the function of the job is has to take place and
> is probably taking place in many quarters. Man has
> to abandon the idea that he has to find meaning in his

job. . . . This does not imply that man is to give up
the idea of work, that is, of meaningful activity. It
means that he must look for such activities in areas
other than the job. Ironically enough, man may have
to find his work in his leisure. . . . As long as
[modern man] holds to the belief that his job has to
give meaning to his life, that he has to define himself
in terms of what he does on the job, he will be in
trouble to the degree that the nature of his job does
not permit him to do so. [27]

In short, this emerging leisure ethic does not deny the symbolic or expressive meaning of work. It simply adds to the work
ethic a vital distinction between work and job. Further, it restricts
the meaning of leisure to those activities that are undertaken freely,
for their own sake. From that standpoint it is not difficult to conclude that when a job does not provide the self-fulfillment that the
individual is seeking, then the job must become instrumental, the
means for the individual to find self-fulfilling work in leisure.

Organizations have, as indicated above, attempted to meet
individuals' needs by various interventions that attempt to improve
the quality of working life. Dubin has suggested that these efforts
may be not only unnecessary but actually counterproductive. Even
middle managers and specialists were able to meet the organization's demands and remain loyal to the formal organizational structure without committing themselves to the organization as their
central life interest.

The source of this organizational confusion may be a sort of
unidimensional thinking, which leads to a belief in multipurpose organizations—organizations in which the goals of the individual and
the goals of the organization can be integrated, in which "concern
for the product" and "concern for people" can be reconciled. [28]

A THEORY OF SOCIAL SYSTEMS DELIMITATION

Alberto Guerreiro Ramos has outlined a theory of social systems delimitation that proposes a "paraeconomic paradigm." This
typology would distinguish between economizing organizations, in
which people earn their income by contributing to the achievement
of the organization's goals, and other types of organizations, in
which people conduct their work/leisure activities and may or may
not earn a living.

Ramos challenges the assumption of extant organizational
theory that the market is the "cardinal category for ordering per-

sonal and social affairs. "[29] The market-centered economy is the
result of a process of derailment by which our classical view of
reason, substantive reason, was displaced by modern, or instrumental, reason. In the classic texts, reason is "a force active in
the psyche of man which enables him to distinguish between good
and evil, false and genuine knowledge, and, therefore to order his
personal and social life. "[30] Modern reason, instrumental rationality, was defined by Thomas Hobbes as a capacity that man acquires
"by industry" and that reduces him to "the reckoning of consequences. "[31]

Our acceptance of the concept of instrumental rationality has
allowed us to lose sight of the fact that the goals of various human
associations may be different. We have accepted the notion that
organizations can pursue a utilitarian purpose and at the same time
provide a vehicle for the actualization of their individual members.
By substituting substantive rationality for instrumental rationality,
it is possible to view the market as a necessary but limited and
regulated social enclave within a "paraeconomic paradigm."

Instead of claiming the possibility of a total integration of individual and organizational goals, the Ramos typology indicates that
human actualization is a complex endeavor that can never be undertaken in a single type of organization. For organizations with a
utilitarian purpose, personal actualization is incidental. In systems
designed for personal actualization, utility maximization is incidental. In the social world described by this typology, there are places
for the individual's actualization free from the prescriptions superimposed by utility-maximizing organizations.[32]

The Paraeconomic Paradigm

Three categories of organizations are described by the typology. They are, of course, to be considered as heuristics or as
ideal types, rather than as descriptions of reality.

Economies are highly prescriptive organizational settings established to produce goods and/or services. An economy possesses
some of the following characteristics: it serves a clientele that
only indirectly affects its planning and decision making; its survival
depends on its effectiveness, which is measurable; it usually is both
large and complex; its members are job holders who are evaluated
on the basis of professional qualifications; and information tends to
circulate asymmetrically among its members, resulting in differential access to information and to power. Examples of economies
include monopolies, competitive firms, nonprofit organizations,
and bureaus.

Isonomies are organized for the express purpose of allowing their members to actualize themselves free from superimposed prescriptions. When prescriptions are unavoidable, they are established by consensus. Members do not earn their livings in an isonomy but accomplish activities that are rewarding in and of themselves. Activities are undertaken primarily as vocations; people work (as part of leisure), rather than labor, in an isonomy. Its decision making and policy making are shared and rotated, and its effectiveness depends on primary relations among its members. For that reason its continued status as an isonomy depends on its remaining below some particular size; beyond that size it will cease to be an isonomy and will take on some other more complex organizational form. Some examples of isonomies are various community-interest groups, student organizations, self-help groups, parent organizations, advocacy groups, some religious and artistic organizations, and consumer co-ops.

Phenomomies are more-or-less-stable organizations initiated and run by an individual or small group and insuring for their members "the maximum degree of personal choice and a minimum degree of subordination to formal operational prescriptions."[33] A phenonomy is characterized as a setting for people to release their creativity in self-selected forms; its members are engaged in self-motivated work, which implies very heavy expenditure of effort and high commitment to the work. The output of the phenonomy may eventually be marketable, but economizing criteria are not what motivate the members. Examples of phenonomies would be associations of artists and artisans, experimental theater and music ensembles, and free-lance artists, writers, journalists, and craftspeople working alone or in various workshop or communal arrangements.

Implications of the Paraeconomic Model

The paraeconomic model implies a conception of production and consumption that formally accounts for both paid and nonpaid activities; it does not equate "productive individual" with "job holder." It also avoids the fallacy of assuming that the amount and quality of citizens' consumption is expressed in what they buy. The prevailing market-centered models, on the other hand, consider as resources or production only inputs and outputs of an economizing nature. As discussed in Chapter 3, Burns has shown that household members who engage in such productive activity as cooking, growing vegetables, caring for the sick, and making household repairs are not considered as contributors to national wealth.[34] Also not considered as resources are the individuals who serve the community by participating in volunteer activities, artistic groups, and educational activities. Burns estimates that the value of the household economy in the United States represents as much as one-half of disposable consumer income.

In considering the human relationship to work and to consumption, Ramos finds that market-centered models assume that "human nature is defined as the set of qualifications and dispositions characteristic of the individual as a jobholder and insatiable buyer."[35] Based on this assumption, individuals are socialized to develop their potential to succeed as job holders and their capacity to prove their worth through the comparative status of their material acquisitions.

The paraeconomic model, on the other hand, assumes that human nature actualizes itself through a wide range of activities, including those that are required through an individual's incidental status as job holder. "Man's actualization is inversely proportional to his consumption of market outputs and commodities and the time required for it. This conception implies that a completely socialized individual is necessarily less than what a healthy person should be."[36]

The significance of this model for the purposes of this chapter becomes clear if we review briefly the emerging trends identified by Yankelovich and Kanter: a changing meaning of success; less concern for traditional status symbols, especially when acquiring them entails sacrifices in terms of lifestyle; a younger, more educated work force, including a greatly increased number of working women; reduced fear of economic insecurity, along with a lessening of role rigidity in marriage (which means increased participation of men in household production); increased rejection of the "cult of efficiency" and rejection of the process of "rationality," or "reckoning of consequences"; and an increase in the psychology of entitlement. The paraeconomic model appears to envision a social world better able to meet the needs of a changing society, a social world that many individuals are coming to consider a right, rather than a wish.


SUMMARY

Organizations may be able to meet both their own goals and the goals of their individual members by separating the two types of goals and applying the organization's resources to the former. Employees can then be given the opportunity to choose, within limits, the amount of time they wish to devote to the activities necessary for consumption and the amount they wish to devote to leisure.

The elements of the argument are as follows:

1. The traditional Protestant work ethic is undergoing significant change. Increasing numbers of employees, both men and women, are seeking jobs that offer intrinsic rewards, jobs that have inherent meaning for the job holder.
2. This change in values is occurring concurrently with changes in traditional roles, particularly with the increased participation of women in the paid labor force and a breakdown in traditional rigid division of household labor between the sexes.
3. There is a trend toward jobs becoming more routinized and repetitive.
4. Organizational theory has not recognized these changes. It continues to assume that employees are men who live in single-career households and are imbued with a traditional work ethic. Further, it is normative to the extent that it seeks to inculcate these values in employees and to reward those who hold them.
5. Organizational theory fails to distinguish between economizing organizations and those organized especially to benefit their members.
6. Organizational theory fails to recognize the distinction between "work" and "job"; hence it assumes that job design or organizational design can address these problems.
7. Some evidence suggests that these efforts may be not only unproductive but, in fact, counterproductive.

Economizing organizations and organizational theorists need to separate the goals of the organization from the expressive goals of the individual. Job design and organizational design methods must concentrate on maximizing productivity. To the extent that flexible, variable work and pay schedules contribute to an organization's efficiency, they are within the appropriate purview of organizational theory—just as job satisfaction, to the extent that it contributes to the organization's effectiveness, is the appropriate concern of the organization.

The employees' need for self-actualization, for meaningful activity, or for personal growth is the proper concern of those organizations created for that purpose: phenonomies and isonomies. Economizing organizations that are genuinely concerned with meeting their employees' need for actualization may find that the most effective way of doing so is to encourage and support participation in family and leisure life. The most productive organizations could well turn out to be those that provide opportunities for their employees to perform to the best of their ability while on the job and opportunities to reduce job time (and income) and devote that time to the leisure activities that have intrinsic meaning for the individual.

NOTES

1. Adriano Tilgher, "Work Through the Ages," in Man, Work and Society: A Sociology of Occupations, ed. Sigmond Nosow and William Forms (New York: Basic Books, 1962).

2. Ibid.

3. Max Weber, The Protestant Ethic and the Spirit of Capitalism (London: Geo. Allen and Unwin, 1930).

4. R. H. Tawney, Religion and the Rise of Capitalism (New York: Harcourt, 1926).

5. Karl Marx, "Alienated Labor," in Man Alone: Alienation in Modern Society, ed. Eric Josephson and Mary Josephson (New York: Dell, 1965).

6. Emile Durkheim, Division of Labor in Society (Glencoe, Ill.: The Free Press, 1947).

7. Rosabeth Moss Kanter, "Work in the New America," Daedalus 107 (Winter 1978):47-78.

8. The following discussion is based on Daniel Yankelovich, "The Meaning of Work," in The Worker and the Job: Coping with Change, ed. Jerome Rosow (Englewood Cliffs, N.J.: Prentice-Hall, 1974), pp. 19-47; cf. Daniel Yankelovich, "Work, Values and the New Breed," in Work in America: The Decade Ahead, ed. Clark Kerr and Jerome Roson (New York: D. Van Nostrand, 1979), pp. 3-26; Daniel Yankelovich, "New Rules in American Life: Searching for Self-Fulfillment in a World Turned Upside Down," Psychology Today, April 1981, pp. 35-91.

9. Ibid.

10. Kanter, "Work in the New America."

11. Ibid.

12. Yankelovich, "The Meaning of Work."

13. Kanter, "Work in the New America."

14. Aristotle, Politics, trans. Ernest Barker (London: Oxford University Press, 1972).

15. Sebastian deGrazia, Of Time, Work and Leisure (New York: Anchor Press, 1964).

16. John R. Kelley, "Work and Leisure: A Simplified Paradigm," Journal of Leisure Research 4 (Winter 1972):50-61.

17. Ibid.

18. John Menefee, "The Economics of Leisure: The Evolution of the Leisure-Labor Trade-off in Economic Doctrines" (Ph.D. diss., Duke University, Department of Economics, 1974), p. 170.

19. Ibid.

20. Ibid.

21. John Neulinger, The Psychology of Leisure: Research Approaches to the Study of Leisure (Springfield, Ill.: Charles C. Thomas, 1974).

22. Ibid.

23. Robert Dubin, "Industrial Worker's Worlds," Social Problems 3 (January 1956):131–42.

24. Ibid.

25. Robert Dubin and Daniel Goldman, "Central Life Interests of Middle Managers and Specialists," Journal of Vocational Behavior 2 (1972):133–41.

26. Ibid.

27. Neulinger, "The Psychology of Leisure," pp. 156–57.

28. Alberto Guerreiro Ramos, "A Theory of Social Systems Delimitation," Administration and Society 8 (August 1976):249–71.

29. Alberto Guerreiro Ramos, "A Critique of Modern Reason" (University of Southern California).

30. Ibid.

31. Ibid.

32. Ramos, "A Theory of Social Systems Delimitation."

33. Ibid.

34. Scott Burns, Home Inc. (New York: Doubleday, 1975).

35. Ramos, "A Theory of Social Systems Delimitation."

36. Ibid.

# PART II

The Practice of
Voluntary, Flexible
Reduced Work Time
for Professionals and
Managers

# 5

## THE INDIVIDUALS AND
## THEIR ORGANIZATIONS

Increased means and increased leisure are the two
civilizers of man.

Disraeli

This chapter and the ensuing ones are based on a study of a
group of professional and managerial employees who have voluntarily reduced their working hours and their salaries, and of the
organizations that employ them. The study was conducted in two
phases. The first phase consisted of interviews with professional
and managerial employees in California state government. For that
part of the study, each of the employees was interviewed along with
his or her supervisor, co-workers, and, where the job entailed
supervision, subordinates. Also, three top managers—department
directors—and eight division chiefs were interviewed.

The second phase of the study consisted of interviews of professional and managerial employees in private-sector organizations
who, like the state employees, have opted to exchange income for
time. In this phase, however, only the employees themselves were
interviewed. In each phase, the interviews followed an open-ended,
unstructured format. A check list was used to ensure that all topics
were covered in each interview. Each interview was tape-recorded
and transcribed for coding and analysis.

The interviews varied in length from one to three hours. They
were conducted in a variety of settings: in offices, in company
cafeterias, over the lunch table, or in executive board rooms. One
took place on the grass under a tree while the subject's young
daughter took her swimming lesson. Another took place "by the
fountain in front of Boalt Hall" (University of California Law School)

where the subject was taking her bar review course. Two were held in the employees' homes.

No attempt was made to collect a representative or random sample of anything. Individuals were asked to participate in the study if they met all of the following criteria:

1. they were professional or managerial employees (or, to put it another way, if they had a high commitment to and investment in a career).

2. they were employed on a salary or hourly wage in a complex organization. Anyone who worked on a free-lance, consulting, or entrepreneurial basis was excluded.

3. they had voluntarily reduced their hours of work and had reduced their pay accordingly.

4. their reduction in hours and pay represented a substantial departure from established practice in their occupation and their organization.

Locating public employees who met these criteria turned out to be a relatively simple task. California state personnel policies and practices permit the use of a reduced time base and the rules governing its implementation are available. Further, personnel policies and practices are a matter of public record and are, within limits, open to public scrutiny. Several departments in state government have permitted limited use of reduced work-time options. Two experimental programs had been conducted earlier—the Shared Position Project and the Part-Time Employment Program. Department managers were quite willing to co-operate in the study; departmental personnel offices were able to provide lists of employees by job classification and time base. Employees were willing, often eager, to participate. The study includes 16 state employees who met the criteria.

Locating private-sector employees who met the criteria proved to be much more difficult. Personnel and industrial-relations offices invariably reported that their companies had no such provisions and no employees on any such program. New Ways to Work, the San Francisco not-for-profit firm that has been in the forefront of job-sharing and permanent part-time programs, was able to provide a list of possible sources from their files. That list, in turn, led to several interested individuals who were able to provide the names of others that they knew about or had heard about. Eventually, this detective work provided 15 individuals who both met the criteria and were willing to participate.

Unlike the state employees, many private-sector employees were ambivalent about participating. In the absence of corporate policies, their schedules had often been worked out on an ad hoc basis with an immediate supervisor. They were very anxious that their situations not be publicized. They were also anxious, understandably, not to make any public statements that might reflect negatively on their employers or suggest that a company policy on the matter existed. For that reason, many of them agreed to participate only if the identity of the organization were concealed. Every effort has been made to present the essence of the findings of the interviews without breaking the promise of confidentiality that was made to every participant.

In all, 15 public-sector and 16 private-sector employees were included in the study. As the networking process proceeded, names were offered for several additional people who might have been included. Conversations were held with some of these people, which helped to corroborate the conclusions and, in some cases, to add new insights.

## CHARACTERISTICS OF THE INDIVIDUALS

If one were to provide a profile of the typical individual who trades away part of his or her income for the opportunity to work less, it would show a woman in her early to mid thirties, a graduate of a prestigious college, possibly with some graduate work, with several years of experience in her chosen career or profession, married to a professional man, with one or two preschool or young school-age children.

That profile could be deceptive, however. To get an overview of the typical short-hour career employee, it's necessary to divide the group into two categories. One would consist of the workers who have chosen to reduce their work time temporarily, usually because of the conflict created by the birth of a child. These people, all women, see themselves as having put their careers on hold. They fully expect to return to full-time work at some future point— anywhere from a year or two to up to eight years. Also included in this category would be the employees, male or female, who have temporarily reduced their work load because they are attending graduate school or because of a temporary disability. This group will be referred to in Chapter 7 as "adapters."

The other category is made up of individuals for whom reduced work time is a way of life, not temporary and not related to other role demands. For these people, reduced work time is an attempt to balance work and leisure, consumption and production, instrumental and expressive needs, in a way that satisfies them. This group is defined in Chapter 7 as "innovators."

Sharon* provides an excellent example of the first category, the employee for whom reduced work time is a temporary accommodation to the demands of the two-career family. She is an officer, an employee, in the world headquarters of a large banking firm in the San Francisco area. She came to the bank seven years ago after graduation from University of California at Berkeley with a degree in industrial psychology. During her early training in the bank's personnel department, she became involved in working with computers. She enjoyed it immensely and has since become very expert in computer applications of personnel functions.

Sharon's husband is a rising young executive in a very conservative firm, also in the financial district in San Francisco. Like the thoroughly modern young couple that they are, they saved their money and bought a dream house in the suburbs, about an hour's distance from San Francisco, and prepared for the birth of their first child.

> Given my particular situation, I wanted to go back to
> the job. I needed to go back to the job—to a job that
> paid X dollars. But at the time I went out on leave, I
> didn't really—I think this happens to a lot of women—
> I didn't estimate what I would feel on coming back to
> work. What do I really want to do? Whether I wanted
> to leave my child? I never faced that before I went on
> leave. I was a professional woman; I would see the
> baby just as much as the father would, etc. Hogwash!
> It was the hardest thing I ever did—going back to work.
> But I had to—financially—or I wouldn't have done it. So
> I figured it out with my husband that after, we hoped,
> three or four months, when we could get our finances
> straightened out, get a few things paid off, car paid
> off, put a little money in the bank, I would work part
> time. I was prepared to take a grade-four teller job
> out in the branch somewhere. That's what I was per-
> fectly willing to do. . . . Grade four tellers on a
> strict salary—I mean given the same hours—they make
> about $700 a month, and I was making $1,500. . . .
> That's just on full-time, and I was prepared to take
> less because I wanted part-time. I was prepared to
> take the absolute minimum. One of the reasons I was
> willing to do that was because the bank's benefits for

---

*All names have been changed.

part-time people are excellent. I've got a loan rate
from the bank, they offer an employee a loan on a house
that is one and a quarter points below the going rate at
the time you take the loan out. Well, right now my
loan is at 7 and 3/4 percent. You don't give that up.
Also, I was able to get medical benefits for $10 more
than I was paying as a full-time employee. Now those
are two terrific benefits . . . if I was going to work it
would be worth it for me to stay with the bank. . . .
So I was prepared to do that. I came back around the
first of November—I wanted to give it the old college
try . . . but with my gut I knew that I couldn't. For me
it didn't work. For some women I'm sure it does and
if you want to do it you can. . . . So around the first
of November I put in a transfer request, because I
knew it took some time and I knew I had to be flexible
in order to get a job out of my branch.

Because of Sharon's computer skills and her competence in
areas where the bank was short on experienced people, her manager
proposed an alternative to her plan to transfer to the branch office.

John basically went to bat—to the head of personnel—
and said, "I want to keep her." Head personnel does
not like part-time officers . . . he really went out on
a limb for me and I appreciate that. It makes you
really feel good that someone will do that for you. He
offered me a job. I was making $1,500 at the time,
and the job he offered me on a full-time basis was
about $1,100 a month. . . . He said, "What kind of
hours do you want?" He left it right open: "What do
you want to do?" I told him that I would like to work
two to three days, and a lot of hours on the days that
I work. So we worked it out—18 hours a week, three
days a week, six hours a day.

If Sharon continues to be "typical" of this group, she will have
another baby within the next year or two and return again to work on
a reduced-time basis. As her children reach school age she'll face
the dilemma of deciding when, or if, to return to full-time work.
She will become increasingly involved not only in activities surround-
ing her children's lives, but in community, social, educational, or
creative activities of her own. She will have to forgo many of those
activities if she returns to full-time work; if she doesn't she will
find her career increasingly lagging behind others in the organization.
Either decision will involve sacrifices and trade-offs.

Janice, on the other hand, approached the decision to reduce her hours slowly and methodically. Now a first-level manager in state service, she works four days a week, a schedule that she adopted three years ago while in an analyst position.

Janice graduated from University of California at Davis and entered state service shortly thereafter. She entered in a professional classification and was promoted rapidly through the ranks. She enjoyed her work and worked hard.

Like Sharon, Janice married after she had started her career and, also like Sharon, she and her husband saved up for their dream house. However, Janice has no children and no plans for them for the present. Nevertheless, she eventually began thinking about reducing her time base.

> When you both work full time and you're together on
> the weekends, and you have a need to be alone—as I do—
> It's hard to get alone.

She first discussed the idea with her husband. He immediately foresaw that among the other benefits would be the increased time Janice could spend catering to his needs, a prospect that he found very appealing.

She was the first professional in her department to request a reduced time base, and the proposal was met with some apprehension.

> My supervisor's first reaction was "My gawd, let me
> take this to [the assistant division chief]. Do you
> realize what this means to your career?" It went all
> the way up to the executive office [and to the State
> Personnel Board] then back down again. No one said,
> "No, we can't do it." Then there was an agreement
> that I would start in August of that year [1976], under-
> standing that it wasn't permanent. We'd see how it
> worked out. "We're doing this because you have a
> good work record—we think if anyone can do it you
> can—but it's not permanent."

A lot of people echoed her supervisor's concern for the damage that she might be doing to her career. She, of course, recognized the risks that she was taking.

> I just didn't know how much. Would it mean anything
> in an examination? It was new. People didn't know
> what to think of an analyst who works less than five
> days a week. Are they truly good? Truly devoted?

Worth promoting? It's the new part that scared people, and they wanted to warn me.

But at the time promotion was not the goal in my life—I wanted to be more satisfied with the balance of my work and personal life.

Janice didn't have a "socially acceptable" reason to make her request so "one was made up."

I didn't have the usual "noble" reasons for working less than full time—family, school, important personal project—so one was fabricated. We were building our house, and I said I needed the time to run errands and do all those things. This was offered as a rationale and seemed to be accepted by management. One said, "I can see how that's a pretty good reason to be taking time off"—so it was adopted to some extent and used.

This reason was not really a consideration in her decision, nor was it a consideration in her being granted the request, but it did offer validity and was included in management's announcement to the organization. Her real reasons were strictly personal.

The additional 20 percent pay just wasn't worth the extra time. I spent so much time on weekends doing errands and all. Now I can do these things on Friday when the crowds are smaller and the lines are shorter.

Mostly, though, it's "time to herself."

I do things around the yard. I cater to my husband—cooking—I never cooked, and he loves it. He loves the attention—errands for him, for special projects. But I don't do housework. I discovered early on that I'd rather work than do housework—I hire someone to do it. I visit friends—a lot of personal time, time to myself, time I never had before. It's very, very important. . . . I have these hours to myself—I love to swim—for exercise, so I go to the pool early in the morning, do laps, sit and read, visit with a girl friend in the Jacuzzi—and I never did that before—then go on to my errands, then pick Bill up. It adds a lot to the quality of my life and to his.

Contrary to the expectations of her supervisors, she has been promoted. Being a part-time worker apparently had no adverse impact on her eligibility for promotion. After she "made the list" she was asked several times if she would like to be interviewed for management jobs, and she refused.

> I wasn't really interested until this job came up. Pro-
> motion was not the goal. But this job provided exposure
> to [some work experience that she considered valuable].
> I finally decided that I shouldn't look a gift horse in the
> mouth. I said I would take it on my conditions—a four-
> day week. They agreed to that—and now I really feel
> that I'm getting the best of both worlds.

Janice cannot perceive a time or an event that would induce her to return to full-time work. On the contrary, she hopes soon to be able—financially—to cut back to three days. However, she doesn't foresee a time when she would stop working altogether.

> I need the mix—the stimulation, responsibility, the
> mental challenge. I couldn't get that at home. . . .
> When I got out of college and started to work . . . I
> was very career-oriented. I'd worked hard and
> studied hard in college. I had no outside interests—
> I preferred to work. I was super-compulsive—study-
> oriented, no hobbies—just wanted to get into a career.
> I even kind of dreaded holidays. Now I'm in a much
> more satisfying stage.

The profiles of Sharon and Janice represent the two categories of professional and managerial employees who choose to trade income for time. While each of the participants in the study can be said to fall into one or the other general category, there are also significant variations within the groups. The remainder of this chapter summarizes the similarities and differences in their general characteristics.

Gender, Age, and Marital Status

Of the 31 subjects, 28 are women. Only five of the subjects are over age 40. Two of those five are men. Twenty-seven of them are married; one is divorced (male); and three are single (including one male). Eleven have no children, two have grown children, and 18 have preschool-age children or young school-age children.

Education

Two of the group—both women—hold law degrees. Seven of them—all women—hold master's degrees, among them two M.B.A.s. One of the men is currently working on an M.A. in psychology. Among other members of the group, seven—including all three men—have earned baccalaureate degrees, and several have done postgraduate study. Six—all women—completed a high school education but no further educational stage. Several of these attended college but have not completed a degree.

Their spouses are also a highly educated group. The 27 spouses hold degrees including four law degrees, three M.B.A.s, three M.A.s, one Ph.D., and 13 bachelor's degrees.

Positions

Occupations and positions vary so greatly that it is difficult to summarize them. The highest-ranking position covered is probably deputy director of a state agency. That position is shared by two women, one of whom is included in the study.

Eight of the participants have supervisory duties; the number supervised varies from one to 26. Public-sector organizations employ seven of the eight supervisors. Thirteen of the participants are in staff positions, doing primarily work that involves relatively long lead times, discrete projects, or autonomous performance. Thirteen are in line positions.

Schedules

All but one of those in the study have opted for either a shorter work week or shorter work days. Six of the private-sector and four of the public-sector employees work every day for from four to six hours. Nine in the private sector and 11 in the public sector work shorter work weeks; for example, two and a half days, three days, or four days, with at least one full day off.

The lone exception is a man who works a full week on alternate weeks—one week on, one week off. Two other schedules that have been implemented by people who were not included in the study suggest some of the creative possibilities. Two men, each working in engineering-based organizations, are experimenting with half-year schedules—six months of full-time work and six months of leave. (These two are not in the same organizations—

neither person is currently on that schedule.) In another interesting
schedule innovation, a group of six attorneys—all male—in California state service "share" five positions, so that each person takes
two months of nonwork time each year.

All of the public-sector and 13 of the private-sector employees work half time or more. The exceptions are a woman who works
two five-hour days a week and a man who works two eight-hour days
per week.

In general characteristics, then, we can say that these people
are alike in that they are young, well-educated, married, ambitious,
successful, and energetic. However, some interesting differences
exist among them in terms of their relationships to their employers,
their families, their communities, and themselves. Those differences will be explored in depth in the following chapters.

## CHARACTERISTICS OF THE ORGANIZATIONS

As with the selection of individuals to participate in the study,
no attempt was made to select organizations that would represent
a random or representative sample of organizations. The search
for participants centered on individuals, rather than on organizations. More or less by serendipity, however, the organizations
that did produce subjects for the study provide a wide spectrum of
organizational types.

Fourteen organizations are represented. Five of these are
public-sector, all in California state government. Eight firms are
private-sector organizations; one is in the not-for-profit sector.
They differ a good deal in size and by industry and are quite similar
in structure.

### Size

In terms of size there is considerable variety. Of the five
departments in California state government, two are extremely
large, with more than 10,000 employees; two are of moderate size,
with 600 to 2,000 employees; and one is quite small—less than 50
employees.

The not-for-profit organization employs 22 people, many of
them part-time, and also makes use of student interns.

In the private sector, all of the firms would be classified as
large. Five are very large by any measure; each, in fact, is a
Fortune 500 company. The other three are somewhat smaller and
newer organizations, but each of these, coincidentally, has been
absorbed by a large conglomerate.

Industry

The private-sector firms represent a diverse array of industries. Two are financial institutions—banking and insurance. Three are manufacturers—two of electronic products, one of food products. One is an international engineering and heavy-construction firm, and one firm is a publisher of shelter books and magazines.

Structure

Structure of organizations tends to be related to size, and so it is not surprising that these organizations, most of which are very large, are also mostly quite mechanistic. They are highly centralized, highly formalized, and highly bureaucratic in nature. Any differences in structure tend to become apparent at the subunit level and, again not surprisingly, the majority of the subjects worked in subunits that were considerably more organic than the larger organization. No differences are apparent between the public and the private sector in terms of the degree of bureaucratization.

What was apparent, and surprising, was the degree of innovativeness on the issue of reduced work time. While state employees, and the public at large, tend to think of public institutions as being much more resistant to change than the private sector, on this issue the reverse is true. The practice of reducing work time for professional and managerial employees in state government is hardly common or widely accepted; yet it comes much closer to wide use and acceptance than is true in the private sector. Despite all the literature and discussion in management literature, it is apparent that almost nothing is being done in the private sector of the economy.

RECAPITULATION

This study includes 31 individuals from 14 organizations. The subjects have in common the fact that each is a professional or managerial employee with a considerable investment in a career, by virtue of either education or experience; each is a salaried employee in a complex organization; each has voluntarily chosen to reduce his or her working time and salary.

The modal-class employee in this group is a young woman with a high level of education and a successful career, who is married to a successful and well-educated man and has one or two small children. However, there are many variations of and departures from this mode.

Of the 14 organizations represented, five are in California state government, eight are in the private sector, and one is a not-for-profit professional association. Twelve of the 14 are very large or are affiliates of very large and highly institutionalized organizations. They represent a full spectrum of business and industrial categories.

# 6

## THE PSYCHOLOGICAL CONTRACT
## AND THE FORMAL ORGANIZATION

They talk of the dignity of work. Bosh. The dignity
is in leisure.

> Herman Melville

Blessed is he who has found his work; let him ask
no other blessedness. He has a work, a life-
purpose; he has found it and will follow it.

> Thomas Carlyle

The ensuing narrative is a descriptive analysis of the experience and insights of the people in the study, using the concept of a
"psychological contract" as a way of ordering the presentation. A
psychological contract consists of the set of expectations, often un-
written and implicit, that employees have of their organizations and
that organizations have of their employees.[1]

John Paul Kotter, in researching the turnover among recent
M.B.A. graduates, found that the important concept in the psychological contract was the number of "matches" between employer and
employee. Getting more or less of a particular expectation was not
as important as whether the employee and the employer each perceived that the expectation was included in the contract at all.
Kotter found that the number of matches of employer and employee
expectations was positively correlated with greater job satisfaction,
productivity, and reduced turnover.[2]

Levinson et al. have identified five types of expectations that
make up a psychological contract: normative, cultural, work-role,
social, and economic.[3] This chapter addresses those elements of
the contract that affect the formal organization: normative, work-

role, and economic expectations. Chapter 7 will look at the contract
that exists between the individual and the informal organization, that
is, the cultural and social expectations.

## NORMATIVE EXPECTATIONS

Normative expectations are arrived at through joint experience
between employers and employees. They include management's expectations of workers and worker's expectations of management.

Aside from the particular norms that exist within specific
professions and organizations, there are some universal norms for
professional and managerial employees in complex organizations.
There is almost universal agreement that employees will behave in
a professional way, that they will demonstrate their professionalism by giving unstintingly of their time, and that, in return, they
will receive equitable treatment from the organization.

### Norms of Professionalism

Being professional means acting in a mature and responsible
way, as well as being committed, loyal to the organization and the
profession, self-motivated, and rational. As women have moved
into the professional and managerial ranks of organizations, the
norms of professionalism have been applied to them equally.

Without exception, the employees in the study had a match on
this point; each is considered to be an outstanding performer in his
or her organization. A good example of the professionalism of
these employees is Kate.

Kate is an associate analyst in California state service. (An
associate analyst is the highest rank in the professional series; her
next promotion will be into management.) She entered state service
nine years ago as a part-time clerk-typist. During her college
years she worked 30 hours a week and carried 18 units per semester. After graduation—with a B.A. in history—she was promoted
to staff services analyst, the first step in the professional series.
With one short break she has worked in the same department ever
since, doing highly technical classification and salary analysis.
She is very good at what she does.

I'm quicker. I organize my time better, and I'm
very experienced. I know all the shortcuts.

Her reward from the organization for her high level of performance
was a heavier work load. Three years ago she found herself in-

creasingly frustrated, unable to keep up with the pace of the work and unable to do the quality of work that she considers acceptable.

In analyzing the situation, she found that her work load had been doubled in the preceding year. She was getting not only the most strenuous assignments but also the most politically sensitive ones, "Jerry Brown's pet projects." She was experiencing "burn-out" at 29 years of age.

Thinking a change of assignment was in order, she applied for and got a transfer to another department. She was dismayed to find that she was bored to death.

> I had nothing worthwhile to do. It was too simple, too routine. There was not enough to do to keep busy. If you answered one letter a day that was enough. I realized that what I really needed was a reasonable work load at what I was good at.

Kate requested a return to her original department on a four-day schedule; her request was granted within an hour. She now works Monday through Thursday and carries a full assignment. She works "full-out" while she is on the job. Now she is able to produce the quantity and quality of work that meet her own standards, and she uses Fridays to do the things that are important to her away from the job. She believes that she has "the very best of both worlds."

Kate safeguards her arrangement. She makes sure that when she leaves on Thursday no loose ends are left for someone else to tie up. If something important turns up, she can come in on Friday and take another day off.

> You have to do your share—you have to carry your end of the load. It's a privilege to be able to do this, it's not a right. You have to treat it that way.

This notion of safeguarding the privilege was repeated over and over again by others.

> I always tell them they can call me at home if anything comes up while I'm gone. They don't call very often, but I always make sure that they understand that it's all right to do that. [an attorney in a public utility firm]

> I've really bent over backward to make it work. I knew that management was really watching. I knew

that if somehow I screwed up, that it would be a long
time before anyone got the chance again. [a manager
in state service]

Unfortunately, perhaps, these people haven't yet been able to
erase the notion that professional and managerial work is a full-
time-or-more role. They are often seen as exceptional cases, so
that even when they have been successful, management may be reluctant to broaden the opportunities for reduced work time.

Delores, an officer in a San Francisco bank, took a leave of
absence to attend law school. After her first year she requested
and was granted the opportunity to work full time during summer
break. She so enjoyed the work she was doing that she requested
and was granted the opportunity to work half time during the fall
semester. However, when she requested a transfer into her department's legal section, in order to apply some of her newly ac-
quired legal knowledge, the request was denied. The reason she
was given, informally, was that the section chief just felt that it
was "unprofessional" for officers to work part time.

Women may be particularly vulnerable to charges of lack of
professionalism. One supervisor in state government, for instance,
was approached by two analysts, both women, with a proposal that
they share a position. Even though he was facing the loss of one
position, which would have meant an involuntary transfer for someone in his unit, he resisted the idea. His comment to his supervisor was:

These women all want upward mobility. They want
the good jobs. But when they get promoted then they
only want to work part time. They aren't really
serious about having careers—they just can't cut it.

Apparently employers and employees agree on a norm of professionalism, and on what that means, but there is some disagreement
about whether one can be professional on a shortened schedule.

The Norm of Time

A norm closely related to professionalism has to do with the
concept of time in professional and managerial work. The concept
of time as money or as a commodity is vital here. These employees
are different from rank-and-file employees—they are exempt from
some of the limitations (and also some of the benefits) of lower-
level employees. They are, in general, free from the necessity of

punching a clock or accounting strictly for their time; but the flip
side of that freedom is that they are expected not to hoard their
time—not to "watch the clock."

For the most part, the subjects understand and accept the importance of this norm. A woman manager in a large insurance firm
made this observation:

> In a place where I worked before, there was a woman
> attorney who worked half time—Monday, Tuesday, and
> a half day on Wednesday. At noon on Wednesday, she
> would walk out of her office, lock the door, and call
> out "Have a nice weekend." You just can't do that!
> It caused a lot of resentment. And when she came
> back on Monday morning, she didn't know what had
> happened while she was gone. . . . I've arranged my
> schedule so that I'm never gone for more than one full
> day at a time. You can manage that. Nobody is here
> all the time—they're out meeting with clients or meet-
> ing with management, or at a Rotary lunch . . . so
> they don't really notice that I'm gone.

The issue is not a simple one, though. How much is enough?
How much is too much? A few people were adamant about working
their assigned hours and no more.

> Absolutely not! No way! I work as hard as I can
> work while I'm here. But I do not take work home
> with me, and I do not come in on my days off. . . .
> They can call me at home if they want to, 'cause I
> won't be there. [a bank officer]

That statement was unusual. More common were comments like
this one:

> Well, I come in if I think it's important. Sometimes
> I can switch my days off, if necessary. I wouldn't
> come in just for a staff meeting. But there is a
> training course coming up and I'll need to have it if
> I want to take on some new kinds of work that I'm
> interested in learning. It's being offered on Friday
> this time, so I'll let it pass. But if it's on a Friday
> next time, I'll come in. [an analyst in state service]

For at least one person, the problem that arose was not a
question of her willingness to work over the minimum, but of the

relationship between her schedule and her professionalism. Marilyn
is the director of the governmental relations division of an association of health-care professionals. She holds a master's degree in
public-health education, is a former Peace Corps volunteer, and
has had a long career in community and public-health work. When
she decided to reduce her work load by sharing the directorship
position with the woman who was her assistant director, most of
the organization, including the manager, looked on the arrangement
favorably. However, one co-worker was visibly upset.

> She approached me one day shortly after—either before
> or after we started and stated . . . I can't remember
> all of it, but the gist of it was that in this kind of job
> you are required to be there when the happenings are
> taking place that demand your attention and input, and
> that might mean hearings at the Department of Health,
> or meetings and hearings at the legislature, or—you
> know—just making contacts, the things you do in a pro-
> fessional, full-time career position where you are
> taking it very seriously and you are always there where
> the action is. The funny thing about that is I agree with
> her. And that is a conflict for me. I feel ambivalent
> about doing my job as well as it could be done. On the
> other hand, how much can you give to a job? But she
> had problems with the fact that I was required to be
> there. And another interesting point which she brought
> up was—you see, you have to understand—she is making
> tremendous inroads in our organization as a legislative
> advocate, a lobbyist, a representative for a profession
> as a woman, as a young woman—in the legislature—com-
> peting with all the other lobbyists who have been around
> forever and are making $100,000 a year. She is push-
> ing ahead as far as her salary requirements go and
> the seriousness with which the organization takes her
> as a professional. And she has done very well! She
> has been there almost four years. I think she is an
> excellent spokesperson for the organization. I think
> she does a tremendous job. I think she deserves all
> the salary, and all the . . . personal accolades that
> she can get and that they give her. And then she
> said, "How can I get this organization to take me
> seriously as a woman and as a professional when
> people like you come in and say, "I want to be a pro-
> fessional, but I also want to go swimming with my
> daughter. I also want to go home and run my
> Brownie troop."

What is involved here is not the employees' willingness or ability to do the work, or the relationship between the time that they are paid for and the time that they work. What seems to be involved is the symbolic meaning of time, the employees' willingness to _invest_ time in the career. This perception probably keeps many employees from requesting a reduced time base. In spite of the evidence that significant numbers of employees, in every age and occupational category, would choose to trade some portion of present or future income for some additional nonwork time,[4] management and co-workers apparently consistently doubt that conclusion. A very typical management comment is:

> My employees are all very career-oriented. I'm sure
> that none of them would be interested in something
> like this.

If management sees reduced time as antithetical to professionalism, then obviously employees are going to be very reluctant to request such a schedule—and if no one makes such a request, management continues to conclude that no one is interested. There may be a mismatch here far greater than many managers suspect.

Norms of Equity

While management is concerned with norms of professionalism or of dedication, employees also have norms regarding equity. Only one of the private-sector organizations has an articulated policy about reduced work time for career employees. Although California has since enacted a comprehensive law on reduced work time,[5] at the time of the interviews there was no express policy about opportunity. Requests have been accepted or rejected on a case-by-case basis, with no criteria established. In general, requests have tended to be granted when the individual making the request is a highly regarded employee. As a result, granting such a request has come to be seen as a reward for high-performing employees in a system that provides managers with very little discretion in rewarding employees.

One manager, at least, phrased his opposition to the whole idea on this very basis.

> It's hard to be enthusiastic about something like this.
> What we have been doing seems to work fine. And
> every time you start something like this, you don't
> know where it's going to stop. How do you keep it

under control? Where does it end? It's always
tempting to try to keep things the way they are.

Some concerned managers ask, "Where will it end?" Other managers, in the same organization, are asserting that "our employees
wouldn't be interested." Obviously, however, some are interested,
and privileges for some come very soon to be perceived as rights
for all.

Cheryl, like Kate, has been a state employee for a number of
years. She started as an intern while in college and entered the
professional series upon graduation. She moved very quickly
through the promotional steps and into management. She had been
a first-level manager for two years and was on the promotional list
to the second level when she went on maternity leave in July 1979.
She had supervised the preparation of the report of the Shared Position Project (described in Chapter 8) and had followed closely the
experience of others in the organization who had reduced their time
bases. Before she left on maternity leave she made it known that
she hoped to return on a four-day schedule.

Although she had not made a formal request, she received a
formal denial, in the form of a memo written by her supervisor at
the direction of the division chief. It said, in effect, that she would
not be permitted to work anywhere in that division on a part-time
basis.

> I was interested primarily because I had a family com-
> ing, but also, I no longer felt that I had to prove any-
> thing. I knew I was competent, that I had proven that
> to myself. I'm a singer by avocation, and I wanted to
> get more into performing . . . there are other things
> in my life, in addition to my career here, that I would
> like to be pursuing.
>
> I went to see the division chief about it. He
> said he had had experience with a shared clerical
> position and it hadn't worked out at all . . . it was a
> real mind set at that time that reduced work time
> meant a shared position.

Angry and upset about what she believed to be an injustice,
she went on maternity leave and didn't pursue the matter further at
that point. The possibility still existed that she could come back in
another division on a reduced time base. However, she contacted
the department's personnel officer when she was ready to return to
work and was told that if she wanted to work four days a week, she
would have to take a voluntary demotion.

> I had always been such a good employee and always
> diligent and had always been told, "Oh, you have such
> a good reputation." I thought about it, and I thought,
> "Fooey—I've worked too hard and too long, and nobody
> knows when they see your employment record why you
> took a voluntary demotion. It looks bad."

The deputy director of the department tried to reassure her. She did, in fact, have a good reputation, she was told, and if she should decide to take a voluntary demotion she would certainly receive consideration for any management positions that came up in the future,

> "assuming that you perform in the future as you have
> in the past." And I said, "Well, I don't see any rea-
> son why I shouldn't." . . . And he said, "Oh, I'm
> sure, I'm sure you would."
> I was bitter, knowing what had happened to other
> people and thinking, "Isn't my reputation as good as
> theirs?" Is my reputation as Little Miss Nice Guy
> who never fights anything? Just goes along with the
> organization?

After much consideration, Cheryl and her husband decided the best strategy was for her to return to full-time work as a manager, hard as that would be on her, and to continue to pursue opportunities for a reduced work load at the manager level. Eventually, she was able to do that, and is now working four days a week, while supervising a staff of three analysts and one technician. When her request was finally granted, only her hours and her salary were reduced; her work load remained the same.

It took an enormous amount of stamina and persistence for Cheryl to get the opportunity that she felt she deserved, and even after management had committed itself to granting her request, there were problems in getting it implemented. In the process "a lot of feathers got ruffled." However, since she began her new schedule, two additional opportunities have arisen that would have allowed her to work at her present rank and on her preferred schedule.

Several mismatches in the psychological contract are apparent here. Cheryl matches management's expectations that career employees will demonstrate professionalism through hard work, loyalty, and achievement. That she has always done so in the past is apparent from her success in the organization. However, her commitment and her continued high performance were questioned when she requested a reduced schedule.

Cheryl and the organization have a mismatch on norms of equity. She expected that she would have the same privileges as others in the organization. When her request was denied, two issues were involved: her rights and her reputation. On one hand, it became clear that the "privilege" had now become a "right," an entitlement for high performers in the organization. In that case, the refusal constituted a judgment of her performance and her reputation. Cheryl had to conclude either that her expectation of equity was not being met or that her performance was less satisfactory than she had always been led to believe. Neither choice was acceptable to her.

Management in state government is still struggling with these issues. In January 1981, after this incident occurred, S.B. 1859 (Rains), The Reduced Work Time Act of 1980, went into effect. This legislation establishes the right of employees to request a reduction in their time base and requires management to grant the request whenever it is administratively feasible.[6] Employees whose requests are refused must receive a written notice with the reasons for refusal, and employees who feel their requests have been unreasonably denied have grievance rights. The State Personnel Board is currently writing the rules and procedures to implement the law. Nevertheless, it will no doubt take some time for the state's management and employees to arrive at a consensus on what is or is not administratively feasible.

In the meantime, managers in state government can anticipate further disruptions. As the idea of reducing hours has spread through state service, more and more employees are requesting, or planning to request, reduced time. Like Cheryl, they are less and less willing to forgo the chance, since others have successfully reduced their work time without detriment to their agencies' or departments' missions.

In the private-sector firms in the study, there was considerably less evidence of the perception of reduced time as an entitlement, probably because so far the practice is less widespread. However, management there, too, may need to consider the necessity for developing and implementing a policy before one emerges incrementally.


WORK-ROLE EXPECTATIONS

Work-role expectations include the employee's perception of his or her own abilities and the way in which the organization uses and recognizes those abilities. Each of the employees in the group studied is, without exception, a highly motivated individual. The

high level of educational achievement among them is indicative of
their high level of aspiration. Each of them, with or without advanced degrees, has achieved an enviable occupational status.

The universal work-role expectations among this group include continued professional growth, tasks that are challenging and
inherently worth doing, and the opportunity to achieve a sense of
accomplishment and recognition. There is a match with their re-
spective organizations on this point, as well as with the expectation
that reducing one's time base will require some sacrifices and some
compromises.

There is some disparity in attitudes about promotion. The
adapters, those who perceive their present schedules as temporary,
are quite willing to make trade-offs for the time being, accepting
the fact that for the moment some opportunities are not available to
them. However, among the innovators, who look on reduced schedules as a permanent lifestyle, there is some concern that they are
not able to compete on an equal basis.

In terms of what constitutes an adequate use of their abilities,
the subjects gave quite consistent answers. Delores's views in this
area are representative of the group. She graduated from a liberal
arts college in New England.

> It's not an Ivy League but it's one of those Eastern
> schools that pretends to be. When pressed we say
> "no," but if someone makes that assumption, we
> don't deny it. I feel legitimate just going along.

She had a double major, in social relations—anthropology,
sociology, and social psychology—and in English. After graduation
she was awarded a Rockefeller fellowship and went to Harvard Divin-
ity School, where she studied theology and ethics.

After one year she left Harvard, for a variety of reasons.
She had decided that she wasn't interested in the ministry as a vocation, she had gotten married, and her husband had dropped out of
law school to follow her to Cambridge. "I wanted basically to get
on with my life and really to work," she says.

They moved to San Francisco; he finished law school while
she began a corporate career. Eventually, she, too, decided to
attend law school, and at the time of the interview was preparing
for the bar exam. She had accepted a position in the real-estate
law section of a San Francisco law firm.

> I never remember thinking of myself other than as a
> professional woman working. I think it was quite a
> shock to me and to most of my friends that I got

married as young as I did, which was right after college. But I knew that that was something different
and in no way signified that it was the end of my professional life. I wasn't dying, I was only getting married. . . . What cemented my decision to go into law
was a strong feeling that it was going to be very difficult to be a corporate woman and ever work on a part-
time basis and be successful the way I wanted to be
successful. And my feelings and observations were
that law was . . . that if it didn't work in one environment it would be more likely to work in another . . .
you have more chance for self-determination. . . .
There's a couple of different areas where you have
lots of client contact. I wasn't interested in the family law practice and wasn't particularly interested in
probate. Real estate, you have a lot of client contact,
so that really helped me to make that kind of decision. For some bizarre reason I loved property law
as a first-year student. I think it's a real character
weakness. . . . My friends from the seminary think
I have just gone amongst thieves, but good. . . . I
had a terrific experience when I was in seminary. I
did a field-work project in the Boston City Jail where
I did pastoral counseling and tutoring of the men that
were in jail, and just watching the counselors and the
social workers and the ministers try to help, I had
just an incredible feeling that they were no help at all
and that the people that were helpful were attorneys.

Delores's expectations are echoed by many of the others, and
most of them also expressed a match on this point.

This is the most interesting job I've had. It offers
independence, intellectuality, the opportunity to exercise judgment and make decisions, to structure
my own time without being hassled. It's a very sat-
isfying job. [a management analyst in state service]

Even when the present situation was less than ideal, the expectation was that the problem was temporary and that things would
improve.

If I felt that I was going to be doing this job the rest
of my life and I would never have anything more challenging to do, I wouldn't like that. But that is not

the situation. [a personnel recruiter in a manufacturing firm]

I like to use my head. I like to make things happen.
That's part of what I like about being a manager.
When I'm here, I like it. Even in these past few
months it's been a relatively negative experience,
I'm learning things and I like it! All day long I like
it! But at one in the morning, I don't like it! [a
manager in state service]

There are, to be sure, limitations that arise from a reduced
schedule. Some jobs simply lend themselves better than others to
schedule variations, particularly when the employee has a particular preference in scheduling.
Ruth, a middle manager in an insurance firm, once supervised 26 employees in a word-processing center. Now, because of
pressing family duties, she works two days a week in the office and
does a great deal of work at home. As she begins to contemplate
increasing her time at work, she considers the options available to
her.

I will never be a first-line supervisor again. Those
people and their problems got to me so much, because I guess I must, in a way, care about people.
I can't take on their problems. You're supposed to do
your job. I mean, I have problems at home and I
come to work, and I have to do my job. So they have
to do their jobs too, but they don't want to do that.
. . . I don't even want to get into that because I
never want to do that again. I want to be responsible
for me only. . . . I have had offers from the personnel office . . . I'd love to work in personnel, but
you couldn't work in personnel only two days a week.
You couldn't work in personnel only three days a
week. . . . I was asked to take a sales position,
which—I love the sales aspect. I love what it is they
want me to sell, it's the personal lines end and working with large corporations to sell them the master
policy. Neat idea. Fun, challenging, a whole new
challenging area, but you can't do that in two days a
week. Not even three . . . contacts and everything. . . .

Recognition is also important to these high achievers, and
that they are not willing to forgo. A manager in state service, who

shares a line-management position with another half-time manager, worries that reducing her hours will somehow make her appear less competent.

> I'd be greatly distressed if having been part-time
> would reduce my competitiveness [for promotion];
> that would be really, really demoralizing. Before I
> went into this my placement was always in the top
> four ranks—fourth rank or above. It would really
> concern me to have it drop. Maybe my performance
> has dropped, but I don't think it has. It would really
> be unfortunate to have someone perceive an artificial
> thing like lowering your time base as also lowering
> your productivity or your ability.

Sarah works in the public-relations department of a large private-sector firm. She has been with the company for ten years and on a reduced time base since the birth of her first child five years ago. She denies that she has been disadvantaged, accepting that she could not be promoted to the next level of management until she was ready to return full time.

> I put blinders on. I want to assume that I am being
> looked at through the work that I am doing and that I
> am being evaluated by the product that I am turning
> out. And by and large that's the way my evaluations
> have been written. There has never been "For a
> part-time person, Sarah has done . . . whatever."
> These evaluations have really been the other way.
> Here is one written by a woman who initially didn't
> want to hire me but did, and she made a comment
> that "Sarah is one of the most competent female man-
> agers I have met. . . ." Now, I couldn't ask for
> anything more. And this is from a woman who has
> a very, very high standard! In another place she
> wrote, "Sarah is a competent manager who has
> emerged as a leader of a major management team."
> Most of the appraisals have been in that way, with no
> mention of the part-time status.

Sarah's first reduced-time job was in the regulatory depart-
ment of the firm, a job that she had never had before. She returned from her maternity leave to a new job, in a new department, on a half-time basis.

It just meant that they had to regulate my work load.
I carried a significant number of cases. I was the
youngest person on the staff, and I can't say that my
work load was exactly equal to the senior people, because they were more used to the complicated issues.
But nobody had to do my work for me, even though I
was working part time.

One of the hazards for part-time people is the lack of lateral
mobility, but Sarah has been fortunate in being able to rotate jobs
periodically.

My boss felt that I was ready to move, and what happened was he treated me like he treated any other employee in the job, and my rotation was supposed to be
after two years and it got closer to three. So then we
put on a marketing campaign. . . . Most of the jobs
I've had, I've had some visibility, and I have a fair
number of people around higher levels who have been
exposed to the work I have done and I think they have
liked what they have seen. So finding a job has never
been a problem for me. . . . So my feeling is there
are so many things a working mother has to juggle,
and I have sort of learned that the jobs come. Now I
don't really worry about where the next job is going
to come from. I feel like I have enough guardian
angels at this point . . . I mean I have enough people
that believe in me, that they are willing to have me
here on a part-time basis. I have learned not to be
afraid to say what I want. I know I run the risk of
being turned down, and until it gets to the point of
"Okay, it is this or nothing," I'm willing to keep going. I've had to sacrifice, though, I have to sacrifice
promotion, but I recognize that. . . . Until I'm willing to declare myself full-time, they will not put me
on a list to be promoted.

The picture that emerges here is of a highly able and ambitious group of people who require jobs that are intrinsically rewarding. They recognize that some jobs that they would like to
have do not lend themselves to a reduced time base, and they accept management's limitations of promotions for workers on a reduced time base.

There is one further situation that requires examination before moving on. In this case, rather than an employee who is

willing to forgo promotion in order to maintain a part-time schedule, we have a person who has committed himself to a reduced time
base as a result of his failure to receive a promotion that both he
and others believed he was entitled to.

Bruce came to California state service as a young man recently released from military service. He is a native of Sacramento and a graduate of California State University. He passed the
state's entry exam with a high score, was interviewed, and started
work within a day or two. His first position was in the Department
of Motor Vehicles as a management analyst.

Bruce was a "fast-track" manager. He worked hard, learned
quickly, and played the part of the swinging bachelor—he drove a
sports car, dated attractive women, and anticipated a successful
career. Management analysis itself, though, was "boring and grim."

In 1969, when "an environmental thing was just beginning to get
started," he transferred to what was then the Division of Highways.

> I, being a country boy at heart, I kind of liked that
> stuff. So I wrote a letter and they hired me, still as
> a management analyst, which was not an appropriate
> class . . . then I was an HAO—a highway administra-
> tive officer—for a while . . . and I dinked around in
> there for a while. But because I was an environmental-
> ist at heart, I didn't fit any of these categories, and
> when the promotional tests started coming along, I be-
> gan to fall in very inopportune places. I would either
> get on a list that was not appropriate for this depart-
> ment, and therefore I could not be hired, or I would
> get way down on the list of a class that I was no longer
> really participating in, like management analysis . . .
> so I was for years without the proper classification,
> so consequently I never got promoted from the day I
> got here, and that was in 1969. . . . I was in the
> director's office under the last administration, and
> working for an exempt position and I had a deputy
> director position—everyone tried to get me promoted
> at one time. They were just trying like crazy to get
> me promoted, but we ran into incredible _____ at
> the personnel board. Inappropriate lists and all that
> sort of stuff. I was on the Governmental Program
> Analyst list, right at the very top, and I couldn't get
> promoted because we had the HAO, which was con-
> sidered an equivalent class. Only I couldn't qualify
> at that list because I didn't do that kind of work. . . .
> It was just one snafu after another and I just finally

gave up. . . . It never did happen. And I've got a
folder up there that is that thick on promotions. There
are letters written by the director and everyone. Oh,
it's just incredible!

To make Bruce's problems more distressing, the department
went through a number of disruptions during this period: a reor-
ganization, a lay-off, and periodic hiring and promotion freezes.

Then something clicked inside here. It just went off,
the circuit finally went off, and I said, "That's it!"
I don't care any more, I gotta do something else. So
I just floated along, vegetated for about a year, really
avoided assignments, did not volunteer for anything,
and that sort of thing.

Gradually the notion of working less than full time became
more and more appealing. He started by using "dock time"—leave
without pay—for a week or two at a time, but it quickly became apparent that that wouldn't meet his needs, and also that it was unfair
to the state, since he would continue to receive full benefits, even
though he was not really working full time.

The solution, finally, was to reduce his time base to half
time, by working every other week (which he calculates as one-
third time, since he works ten days out of every 30). Because of
his seniority in his unit, and perhaps because his department felt
some obligation to him, but most importantly because he is very
good at what he does, he has been able to design his job so that he
makes maximum use of his time, working on the assignments that
interest him the most. He seeks his rewards and his self-fulfillment
in his leisure.

The moral of this sad tale, perhaps, is that a reduced work-
time base is most often seen as a reward for employees who have
demonstrated their commitment and their ability, but who have
chosen to change the balance in their lives. In this case, however,
an ambitious and able employee chose reduced work time because
of his disillusionment with the bureaucratic system. From the public's perspective, it would have been preferable if he had chosen to
remain on the job and continue his high level of performance. It is
also reassuring that he chose to reduce his time and his salary to
an extent commensurate with his reduction in productivity.

The significant conclusion, however, is that in terms of work-
role expectations, this group of employees has a high level of ability, which is recognized by their employers. They expect work that
is challenging and rewarding, and they expect to be recognized for

their contribution. They expect to be evaluated by the same criteria as their full-time colleagues. They recognize, however, that
in order to maintain their chosen schedules they may have to forgo
some opportunities, both for assignment and for promotion.


ECONOMIC EXPECTATIONS

Each of the people interviewed has voluntarily reduced his or
her income in exchange for additional time. This fact, taken alone,
leads some observers to conclude that these are all middle-class
housewives working for some reason other than financial need. To
some extent that's true—many people, clearly, would choose to
work less if they could afford to do so. However, it would be a
gross oversimplification to assume that this is a panel of dilettante
housewives. For many of them, it's true, the loss of income was
not a great financial burden. In some cases, dual paychecks put
the family into such a high tax bracket that the loss of net income
is significantly less than the loss of gross income and amounts to
only a small fraction of household income. In other cases the loss
is inconsequential because the individual or the household members
have chosen a relatively simple lifestyle where less income is required.

For some, however, the loss of income represented a substantial sacrifice. Also, for most, the income has a symbolic
meaning; it's a symbol of recognition and achievement—sometimes
of power within the marriage—and is very important. Obviously,
in every case, the additional time is more important than the loss
of income.


The Explicit Economic Contract

All but three of the subjects have moved from full-time employment to reduced time within the same organization. How the
new salary was determined varied by economic sector. For state
employees, the salary is simply the appropriate percentage of the
full-time salary for the employee's job classification. Under state
employment rules, any employee regularly scheduled to work half
time or more is a member of the State Employees Retirement System (PERS) and is entitled to full health benefits as well. Fringe
benefits for pay for time not worked are prorated. Since these are
exempt employees, there is no overtime pay. Sometimes they can
take compensating time off.

For private-sector employees, the most common approach is to put the employee on an hourly rate that is calculated by dividing the full-time salary by the full-time number of hours. In these cases the most common arrangement is for the employee to keep and submit a record of the hours worked. Of course, there is some contractual agreement about the minimum number of hours per week that the employee will work and under what circumstances that number will be exceeded. However, in two of the private-sector organizations the arrangement is analogous to the state system—the employee works an agreed-upon number of hours for an agreed-upon salary, and extra hours can be taken as compensating time off. Private-sector employees have one major advantage over the state employees in that it is a good deal easier to renegotiate their contract. In state service a renegotiation, particularly to revise the number of hours upwards, must be approved not only by the department and the agency, but also by the department of finance. Under a hiring freeze, a common constraint in contemporary times, that approval is difficult to obtain.

In both private- and public-sector organizations, employees expressed no dissatisfaction with salary as a result of being employed part time.

Only three of the people had been able to obtain employment on a reduced time base without prior full-time employment in the firm. All three were in private-sector organizations. In one of these cases, the salary was negotiated just as it would be for a civil-service employee—that is, a proportion of the full-time salary for that position, plus full fringe benefits. The other two cases represent the two lowest-paid people in the study.

Joan has an M.A. degree in textiles, and credentials that qualify her for college teaching jobs; but none is available to her in the suburban area where she lives with her husband, a Ph.D. physicist, and her two small children. She has been taking courses in accounting and computer science at the local community college. Two years ago, she was asked by a local firm to work on a temporary basis to do an internal audit. She was hired at minimum wage to work 20 hours a week. The simple little internal audit turned out to be "a behemoth." The firm employs about 1,500 people, manufactures sophisticated electronic measuring devices, and is a part of a much larger conglomerate.

When the audit was finished she took on a position in accounts payable. After four months she was handling a full-time position in 20 hours: "Then, in between there I was doing data entry for the computer and getting to know computer work." She now regularly works half days in the computer room.

What you learn to do in the computer room in such a
small shop is everything. So you are analyst, you're a
programmer, and also the operator, plus sometimes you
do data entry—which is very low—but in the interests
of getting the whole thing done, that's what I'm doing
right now. . . . I work strictly in the computer room
20 hours a week and it works out very well. I come in
the morning, I start the machine, I do the initial program load, I pick up time and attendance discs . . .
and I collect all that and I transmit it to corporate,
who handles all our payroll. But we are almost on
line with our payroll here . . . we are going to be
bringing out our own payroll and we are doing data
entry right now for that, to bring it on line, but the
payroll clerk will take over all the menial stuff.
Mostly our job is to trouble-shoot. You have to get
the computer up, explain why it is down, increase
file sizes—mostly maintenance stuff, what a computer programmer would do. . . . I decided that
[accounts payable] could go on the computer really
easy and, in fact, they are giving it a number-one
priority as soon as payroll is on line, which they expect by September 1, and I am really excited about
that because I know our accounts payable systems in-
timately. No one in the computer room does, so I'm
going to be able to get my hands into that, and that is
why . . . I've got the IBM self-study manuals at home
and I'm halfway through them. I'm helping with the
data base for personnel. They were going to hire a
consultant—$1,500 a month to help do that, and I know
that she couldn't do it. They predicted it would take
80 hours. I got everything on with the current value
in 16.

Joan began this job at $3.15 per hour, and now earns $5.40
per hour, and "that's in a year and half, which [her husband] said,
'percentage-wise you are just amazing.'"
Why would Joan do this level of work for so little money?
For a number of reasons: she enjoys the "attaboys"; she enjoys the
stimulation and the sense of accomplishment that comes from
"bringing order out of chaos." Most of all, she enjoys the freedom
and independence that this contract gives her.

I don't have an inflated opinion of myself, but I'm valuable enough around here so I can say what I want to do.

I just told them I'm going to [Washington to visit her
parents] and they said "fine" . . . I just mentioned to
them that I would be gone three weeks instead of two.
"Well, don't leave—just come back." That's what
she said.

An almost opposite approach to negotiating an explicit contract was taken by Carol. The circumstances were similar in some
ways: she was applying for a job in a field where she had little technical expertise, although she, too, has earned an M.A. (in English
literature) and has considerable working experience. She, too, has
a husband with a well-paid job. Carol began her present employment (as an editorial assistant) by finding another woman with whom
she hoped to find a job-sharing position. Under the auspices of New
Ways to Work, they developed and executed a plan that ultimately
came to fruition, and they were offered the job.

On the third interview he hired us. Then we came
down to money . . . I can't explain it. It wasn't exactly a lark, but neither one of us desperately needed
this job. We experimented and it worked. There were
probably some other people that wanted that job and
probably tried very hard. It was just one of those
things. . . . We decided—he offered us something
like—I've forgotten what it was—something like $9,000.
Editorial work is notoriously low-paying . . . at least
on the West Coast, it's terribly low. We didn't know
that at the time. He had said something like $9,000
and we decided that that just simply wasn't enough
money. If we had gotten him this far, we could probably talk him into more. So it was my job, and I'm
really quite shy. It was my job to work it up so that
we had gotten them up to $10,000. . . . She [her
partner] gave the opening phrase that made me have
to say it. . . . We had to build up his ego about it.
It was fun. It was a good show. But anyway, we demanded something and then we could compromise . . .
and afterwards, I think it kind of—it was much more
than they had intended to pay. But they got what they
needed. And we started at $10,400.

Carol and her partner had carefully worked out a proposal for
splitting the fringe benefits, but the company's office manager decided that each should have full benefits. At the time that this contract was negotiated, the firm was an old, established, and rather

small one. It has since been purchased by a conglomerate and formal policies cover these decisions. Over the years Carol and her partner learned more and more, took on considerable editorial responsibility (for a magazine), and gradually increased their hours. They each experimented with various schedules but neither of them has ever exceeded 30 hours a week.

Last year Carol's job-sharing partner left California and she is now the only part-time employee on the editorial side. Salary continues to be an issue. Recently she resigned her position because of a number of problems that she felt were associated with her reduced work-time status, including salary.

> But anyway we came to an understanding . . . and I
> still got the money that I wanted. It was a stick-up.
> I didn't plan that. . . . As it turned out I came back
> [after three days]. It was one of those things where
> I—he kept telling me that he would give me a salary
> increase that I would be pleased with. I don't know
> what he had in mind but when I saw the pay scale, it
> was just a little scrap of paper! Nothing! Just this
> little scrap of paper with salary increases.

Once again, this "shy" person was able to stand her ground and negotiate a salary that she feels represents her value to the company. As in Joan's case, her income is not essential to the family. On the contrary:

> When I quit he [her husband] asked me, "Was it to
> save money?" We would save money if I stayed
> home right now, but I don't want to stay home. . . .
> I don't make enough money to pay for the taxes that
> go out as a result. . . . Either I have to find a
> really dynamic, tremendously good-paying job or
> else just consider this something that I like to do
> and not get too keyed up about the money.

Implicit Contracts

Many of the elements of the psychological contracts represented in the study are inherent in these last two examples. For many, like Joan and Carol, the dollars themselves are not important, since their husbands earn substantial amounts of money; for some others, the dollars themselves are unimportant because their lifestyles don't require a lot of money.

Mary is a single woman in her early thirties, an analyst in state service. Her full-time pay would average about $26,000, and she has reduced her time to two and one-half days a week. She considers this perfectly adequate for her needs.

> I'm still earning more now, half time, than I was when I started full time in state service.

Kate, also an analyst in state service, works four days a week. Her husband has been in school and has recently begun to sell real estate. They have no bills, and they live a "minimal lifestyle." Her reduced pay cut their savings plan in half—a sacrifice they were both willing to make, even though the savings plan is the means to some very important long-range goals. Their recreation most often consists of backpacking or other outdoor activities that incur little expense. Kate and her husband have no children.

Norma, a half-time manager in state service, has a son who graduated from college last year, and she has cut her work time in half. It made little difference financially:

> We were putting $200 a month into the credit union, so going half time reduced my income by only $150. It really didn't change the way we live at all.

Bruce, an environmental planner, also has experienced very little change in lifestyle since he began working half time; he spent three years getting ready. He is a serious amateur photographer, but his plans specifically exclude a second career.

> I take pictures of things that I like and then I have photography shows and galleries and bits and things like that. It's not on a paying basis as yet, but it has some promise of at least paying expenses, if not a salary. That's another important thing. I do not have the intention—the reason I have been planning this for so long is because I wanted to get my finances to a point where I did not feel the need to turn a profit with my free time. I did not have to go moonlight a job some place. If I wanted to do nothing but go for a walk in the woods, that is O.K., and I wouldn't feel guilty about it. So that's why it took me three years— to grind down the charge cards and all that mundane stuff, get the car paid off and get the personal life squared away—so that I don't need a lot of money. There are two ways to get through. You either have

to make the money which will buy you the kind of life
that you think you have to have, or you can change
those expectations and you don't need the money any-
more. And that's what I've done.

Although Bruce is unmarried, he has a living-together arrangement (LTA) with a full-time state employee. She has recently
been promoted, and they handle their money essentially autonomous-
ly. She fully supports his decision; she only asks, "Don't rub it in."
For a number of others, the loss of pay represents a sacrifice, and the feelings of the spouse have some considerable impact
on the employee's ability to adjust to that. One man (a high-ranking
state executive) who, because of a temporary stress-related disability, had worked a variety of reduced work-time schedules, found
himself deeply caught in the expectations of middle-class society.

I would be perfectly happy working half time if my wife
made enough money. She is badly underpaid for the
work that she does. . . . But we've bought into the
upwardly mobile middle-class ethic; with my salary
and both of us working we have a pretty good life—kids
in college, an expensive home, trips to Europe, skiing
vacations, the whole thing. Those expectations would
be dealt a severe blow—she is not willing to give them
up. She has bought into it more than I have. . . .
Then there is the reaction of our parents—our very well-
to-do parents; they strongly disapprove.

This couple, a single-career couple, probably demonstrates
as well as any the dysfunctions of that lifestyle. For dual-career
couples, the responsibility for the family's income is shared by the
wife, and when income loss occurs, she shares the stress. For example, a woman manager, with two preschool children and a teen-
age stepson, has cut her work time in half by sharing her job.

Now we're really hurting for money. My husband has
never said anything. We've talked about it a lot. I've
tried to make sure he doesn't have any trouble with
me working half time. But I don't know that I feel that
I can continue to put that burden on him and on the
whole family. . . . Maybe we could manage on four-
fifths time. You want to have money to do things.
You can't just continue to say, "We'll just scrimp,"
so that I can work half time so that I can be home
with my babies.

In state service, employees have more difficulty than private-sector employees do in readjusting their schedules, should they find the financial burden more oppressive than they had expected. One difficulty apparently unique to public employees is that management and employees often adopt a job-sharing model, rather than any of the other numerous possibilities, because they are unaware of other choices. Job sharing means a half-time job, a very substantial cut in pay. Public employees may also have greater difficulty in either returning to full-time work or increasing their time base.

A job-sharing analyst, with no children but with some very absorbing leisure activities, commented:

> When I was working full time there were so many
> things I wanted to do and couldn't because I didn't
> have the time. But now I can't always afford to do
> those things. I'd like to try three-fifths or four-
> fifths time. There has to be a right combination.

A co-worker of hers, on the other hand, had found the trade-off that worked best for her:

> Right now four-fifths time is the financial threshold,
> having bought a very expensive home and wanting to
> support a lifestyle. When we get some things paid
> off I might go to less time . . . I'll never go back to
> full time. The only reason would be a dire financial
> disaster. Even if I got divorced, I have many inter-
> ests. The extra 20 percent just isn't worth it.

Finally, whether or not the dollars are important, and whether or not the worker and spouse can support whatever lifestyle they have chosen, there is the symbolic meaning that salary has for the individual. The symbolism is important both as a factor in the marriage relationship and as a measure of the individual's own achievement and recognition.

Two women, one in the public sector and one in the private sector, had each worked half time; each has since changed from that schedule (one up, one down). They made almost identical comments.

> As a half-time worker I felt that I was no longer an
> equal partner in the marriage—my husband didn't
> complain and he never threw it up to me, but I didn't
> like the feeling. I was very reluctant to spend any
> money on myself. I no longer felt that I had the right
> to do that.

Marilyn has had a long career in public health and community work, both paid and unpaid, both full-time and part-time. She is particularly articulate about what the salary means to her; she, too, enjoys a comfortable, though not lavish, existence. Her husband is well paid and they live a rather quiet life in the suburbs with their only daughter. So the dollars themselves don't make a big difference, but

> I don't think it [part-time work] affects my job opportunities as much as it affects my salary. If I go anywhere and ask for part-time—if I had done that I was going to state that I needed so much per hour. They could call me a consultant and give me no benefits, which I don't need—or whatever they wanted to do, but I was going to up what I was getting a little bit. And if I ever do that, I will say, "Gee," . . . I will try to psych myself into the fact that I'm worth, if not $30,000 a year prorated, at least what I think I would be earning had I been in a continuous full-time job, prorated. . . . At this point, having been working off and on for 15 years, I'm beginning to say simply—my human relations skills, my job skills, have got to bring me—I have to tell myself that I'm worth it. . . . What happens is that it is demoralizing to me to work for less than I think I am worth. I get excited about a job and think, "Gee, this would be fun. I would enjoy coming to work and doing this." At one point with [her present employer] I said to myself that I would almost pay them to work here, I love it so much. There is no pressure, I get to do what I want, it is rewarding. I just really enjoyed it. But then it got to be a little less enjoyable, sometimes there was more pressure—I was putting up with a little more grief, and I said, "Gee, if I am doing this, I ought to at least be compensated." Good words—"salary" and "compensation"—for what you put up with. But I would tend to go looking for another job and say, "Gee, this looks good, I'll take that salary, it doesn't matter." I have always kind of said that it doesn't matter. But then the first time you get down about the job, and say, "Gee, I am only making this much money and putting in this much effort and taking this much grief—I ought to be making a little bit more." . . . So I think I should be more realistic in going into a job and say, "I think I need and deserve X amount of dollars." That would be good to work out ahead of time . . . I think

> everybody—I think . . . there is an underlying feeling
> that they are getting away with something and maybe
> you don't need it as much . . . if you can work part
> time then you don't need the money so "let's see if we
> can pay her less."

Obviously, these comments reveal a great discrepancy in economic expectations. For some, the dollars themselves are important, and the decision to reduce income represents a substantial sacrifice. For others, the dollars are not important, either because the spouse is the "breadwinner" or because the individual's lifestyle simply doesn't require a big income. Whatever the financial implications, however, the salary has symbolic meaning that is important to each of these people, either because it represents an equal role in the marriage or because it represents recognition and compensation for the contribution to the organization.

In most cases, there is a match on this item. Most of the employees in the study are receiving a prorated share of the amount that they would receive on a full-time basis, and in addition most of them are receiving equal or better fringe benefits. In the private-sector cases where the employee was hired as a part-time professional, there is more of a tendency to underpay, but only one employee out of the group is dissatisfied with her present pay.

One potential hazard for either the organization or the individual in the explicit contracts is that in most cases the salary is negotiated on the basis of time rather than of work load. Since most of the employees are considerably more productive than their full-time counterparts, there is a potential to feel exploited. In fact, however, although most of them agreed that they were underpaid by that measure, they were unconcerned about it. Most of them were high achievers on full time, and they were quite willing to make the extra contribution in exchange for the privilege of adjusting their schedules.

Sarah, for example, who devotes enormous energy to her public-affairs position, refuses to look on herself as victimized.

> Most of the jobs I've done have been full-time jobs
> that I've done on a two-thirds basis. . . . I've either
> filled a specific job that was there, or—in two cases—
> it has been a new job that was added. . . . I keep
> track of the hours. The agreement was that I would
> work 20 hours and anything over 20 I would turn in
> my hours. . . . I take stuff home, but everybody
> does that. I'm not looking to feel exploited. I feel
> that what I wanted was time for my children while they

> are small. . . . And because I am paid for the actual
> hours I'm here, I don't feel exploited. If I was really
> pushed, I would say, "Gee, a lot of people get paid for
> the time they go to the doctor, or when they take ex-
> tended lunches and all that." I am not willing to go and
> pick a fight.

In only one case was an employee genuinely and unacceptably
exploited, and her case is an important one, as an example of the
hazards to both employee and organization. Connie has worked in
state government since 1975, and had worked in a food-services
business in San Francisco for five years before that, earning an
M.B.A. in the evenings. She is energetic, hard-working, and ambitious. Her husband and she, friends from high school, have an
unusually similar background and coalition of interests. Both take
their work very seriously, and each has almost routinely taken work
home from the office. She had made rapid progress through the
ranks in state service and was due for promotion to management
when she went on maternity leave. When she returned from leave
she asked for and got a three-fifths assignment, working Tuesday,
Wednesday, and Thursday.

When she was offered a managerial position in another department, her division chief agreed, reluctantly, to promote her to a
managerial job on a four-day schedule, in order to keep her. After
some hesitation, she agreed that she would give up one day in order
to get the promotion. She hoped that before too long she might be
able to share a manager's position with another person; that would
give her both her promotion and more time with her daughter.

She began on her new job—her first management assignment.
On her very first day, a sensitive political situation arose that affected her unit and that effectively doubled its work load.

> It couldn't have been worse. For pretty much the
> whole month of March a new employee, my supervisor,
> and I tried to put band-aids on all the other work and
> make something happen of this [special project]. It
> was the project that [executive and political branches]
> were interested in. We were told it could not fail—
> yet it was doomed for failure. So we started putting
> in marathon hours.
>     I've always been willing; if something needs to
> be done, I'll do it. But I have at least grown enough
> in my own awareness not to do it willingly. From the
> beginning I was screaming at the top of my lungs,
> saying, "I will not do this"—this was not part of the

bargain. Within a month we were up in the executive
office with me saying, "Hey—I have already put in 70
additional hours in March." Work still had to go
out. . . . Oh, I can't even tell you—it was so painful.
I guess the real difference is I was standing up for my
rights.

Eventually (after three months), a very competent analyst was
rotated into the department to take over the special project. The
next day at a staff meeting it was announced that her supervisor was
also going to devote full time to the special project, and that a new
assignment was being added to her unit.

I was in tears. I said, "You just can't do this to me.
I won't do it. I'll demote! I'll go back to three-
fifths time! I'll leave the organization!"

However, the pattern has continued. Because she is a competent and reliable employee, the organization continues to pile
work on her, in almost total disregard of the fact that she has reduced not only her hours but her salary by 20 percent. In writing
performance standards for her, her supervisor said,

One of your performance standards should be that
you're able to do your work in four days.

She responded,

Then one of yours should be that you don't give me
any more work than I can reasonably do.

At the time of our interview the dilemma had not been resolved.

I feel like a spoiled child. I feel like every inch of
the way I've had to tell them; I feel like their boss,
telling them what's reasonable—what they can expect. I've said to them, "Look, I'll leave; I'm committed to this—I'm committed to making something
work. I'm not setting myself up for failure. I re-
fuse to commit to doing work that is beyond a full-
time job. Understand, I'm willing to put in another
hour or so a day—that's part of the territory—but
I'm not willing to do as I'm doing now, going home
every night and doing four hours of work—and weekends. I'm not going to do it—but then I do it!

Management has promised to take Connie's problem seriously and find a way to keep its commitment to her. In this case it is
not only the psychological but the explicit contract that is being vio-
lated. In the process a highly valued employee is becoming increasingly distrustful of management. Again, it's important to empha-
size that this incident is included here not because it is typical, but
because it is so atypical of what is happening. It does, however,
dramatically demonstrate the hazards of reducing hours without an
adequate renegotiation of the contract.

In the great majority of cases, employees are contributing a
substantially increased amount of work in comparison to their full-
time co-workers. Some are quite aware that this could be considered exploitation, but they are aware that their full-time co-workers
also, from time to time, must make special contributions. Their
economic expectations are a match.

NOTES

1. Harry Levinson, Charlton Price, Kenneth Munden, Harold
Mandle, and Charles Solley, Men, Management and Mental Health
(Cambridge, Mass.: Harvard University Press, 1962).

2. John Paul Kotter, "The Psychological Contract: Managing
the Joining Up Process," California Management Review 15 (Spring
1973):91-99.

3. Levinson et al., Men, Management and Mental Health.

4. Fred Best, Flexible Life Scheduling (New York: Praeger
Special Studies, 1980).

5. Reduced Worktime Act of 1980. California Senate Bill
1859 (Rains).

6. Ibid.

# 7

## THE PSYCHOLOGICAL CONTRACT
## AND THE INFORMAL ORGANIZATION

Nothing is so dear and precious as time.
Rabelais

Chapter 6 reviews the relationship that exists between the
worker and the formal structure of the organization—the normative,
work-role, and economic expectations. Specifically, it reports and
analyzes the expectations of a selected group of workers—professional and managerial employees who have voluntarily reduced their
hours and their pay—by looking at both what those expectations are
and the degree to which those expectations are being met.
Chapter 7 addresses itself to the relationship between the
same group of employees and the informal structure of their organizations. It identifies some of the cultural expectations imposed
upon them by the larger society and assesses the extent to which
they have conformed to, altered, or rejected those expectations.
It also looks at their social expectations, their own expectations
about their sense of acceptance and belonging in the organization,
and the extent to which those expectations are being met. Throughout, the important issue involved is the extent to which these expectations either affect or are affected by the decision to reduce
working hours.

CULTURAL EXPECTATIONS

A basic tenet of this study is that organizations continue to
exert pressure on employees to live up to sex-role expectations
rooted in a social world that no longer exists. Organizations expect

professional and managerial employees to conform to a masculine model of work; that model asserts that the individual's career takes precedence over all other aspects of life and that women who seek successful and fulfilling careers must also meet those expectations. Any adaptation must be on the part of the individual, not on the part of the organization. The society, however, also expects men and women to conform to behavior patterns determined by stereotypes of gender, race, and social class. The extent to which the employees match these cultural expectations is, therefore, of considerable significance.

The group divides into three subgroups. One group, made up of people like Sharon (described in Chapter 5), we have called the adapters; they are responding to the pressures of multiple roles by adaptation or compromise. This group, all women, may be adhering to a new female stereotype, "the Superwoman." They are corporate executives, corporate wives, and middle-class mothers. They keep tightly organized schedules, in order to meet the cultural expectations placed upon them by every role. They have a high level of energy and enthusiasm and seem highly satisfied with their existence, although others would find their schedules exhausting. They have a match, and they consider themselves extremely fortunate to have the opportunity to achieve what they want in all areas. Nevertheless, using the single-career/dual-career typology, they would be considered single-career wives, since they are, at least temporarily, subjugating their own careers to the needs and expectations of their husbands and children. Some of them will return to full-time work; some will leave the labor force altogether.

A second subgroup, which we'll call innovators, consists of people who are more or less self-consciously defining a new set of role expectations. They have not chosen their working schedules as a means of accommodating to the demands of multiple roles; rather, they have chosen them as a way of reordering their own lives. Whether or not they are married or have children, these people look on reduced work time as neither an accommodation nor a temporary phenomenon. They expect to continue to work this way for the rest of their career lives. They may be considering whether to cut back more, but not whether to return to full time. However, they do not anticipate leaving the labor force altogether.

A third group, the rebels, forms a subgroup of the innovators. The rebels are people who experience particularly strong pressures to conform to traditional roles, because of their ethnic background, their marital status, or their social status. In each of their cases, they have overcome the pressures to conform, although not without cost. Each of them, in his or her own way, has struggled to choose an ideal balance of work and personal roles, and some are struggling still. Their future decisions or preferences are indistinct—they are concerned more with the present than with the future. Whatever their choices in the future, they will be made on the basis of individual, rather than cultural or organizational, expectations.

## The Adapters

Beth is probably the most dramatic example of a multiple-career woman: attorney's wife, mother, corporate attorney.

> I was always prepared to go to work, to have a job, that was sort of my expectation. They always compared me to my aunt, who is a noted archeologist. It was always felt that I was just like my aunt and would go far. I went to Harvard and majored in Latin. I did some volunteer teaching and some tutorial work. . . . I realized that there was a lot more to teaching than just a subject that you loved. . . . Now I was very interested in current events and politics and so forth, and said, "What am I doing here in the first century B.C.?"
> Now my father knew a woman lawyer, a very dynamic woman lawyer, who was [name omitted]. . . . So my father arranged for me to meet her, and she was so dynamic and wonderful, and she said law is a wonderful career for a woman, and there are so many opportunities for part-time work. . . . Well, little did I know I was talking to one of the most famous people in the world. At that time she was teaching at Howard University.
> She said, "Absolutely, go to law school, you'll love it." So I applied [to Yale Law School] in my junior year, and I got in and met my husband in my senior year. He was a first-year law student at Harvard. He said, "Look, you don't want to go to Yale"; and I said, "Actually, I do want to go to New Haven! I'm sick of Cambridge, and I've paid my $100." . . . So he proposed to me, we got married, and I went to Harvard.
> He finished Harvard Law School and I had two years at Harvard, and we decided that we wanted to move out to California, so I finished up at the University of California, Berkeley. I did pretty well at law school, slightly better than he did. He was very un-

threatened by that kind of thing. He was just very
proud of me.

When he finished Harvard Law, they decided to leave Cambridge
and move to California, even though she still had another year.
    After her graduation from law school, she followed her hus-
band to Virginia while he did two years of army duty, after which
they returned to California, he to take up the position he had left,
she to find a new position. They spent the next three years as associates in San Francisco law firms, putting in long hours and estab-
lishing their careers.
    When the time came to start a family, Beth suffered two mis-
carriages. She was able to persuade her law firm to let her work
half time during her next pregnancy. The arrangement worked out
happily for all concerned. When her daughter was born she resigned and "went home to raise a family."

> I had decided that I did not want to go right back to
> work. . . . I told them that. I said, "I don't know
> when I want to come back, but not for quite a while,
> so I want to just sort of terminate our relationship,
> and not be on a leave of absence or anything." I
> didn't want to feel any commitment to come back in a
> year or two years. I didn't know what I was going to
> do, but I suspected that I was going to stay home with
> my child.
>     I really enjoyed being home with her, and that was
> what I really wanted to do. One of my former bosses
> had a couple of cases that he couldn't get the firm to
> take, and he got me involved in working on a few of
> those. . . . I established a pro bono rate for myself;
> I wanted to get some money because I had to find a
> babysitter, and I had the expense of maintaining my
> bar association membership. So I didn't work . . .
> but I worked at a pro bono rate and kept my hand in.
> It was all very low-key; it wasn't very many hours a
> week, and that was enjoyable. . . . Time passed
> and we had another baby.

When her children were two and four, respectively, Beth decided to return to her practice of law on a half-time basis. She
discovered that the advice she had received years ago, that there
were lots of part-time opportunities, was misleading. The firm
that she had left so happily four years before refused to hire her
back on a half-time basis. She was referred to the partner in

charge of hiring law students as interns—a painful put-down for
someone with her credentials. She eventually found her present
position on the legal staff of a public-utility firm, a job she loves.
Here she is highly respected, and she can work half days. Her
career progress is slower than it might otherwise be, both because
of her reduced time base and because of her lack of geographical
mobility; but these trade-offs she makes quite happily. Her days
are a mosaic of job duties and family activities: car pools, baby-
sitters, doctor's appointments, school events—all of the responsibilities of a mother of two young children.

What of her husband, while she is doing this juggling act?

Well, we have started to go off together on little trips—
which we didn't until quite recently. . . . He does not
spend much time with the children. If there is a flaw
in the current situation, it is that he works very hard,
very long, and somehow can't seem to delegate the
work, or maybe he has too much to delegate, or maybe he doesn't have anybody to delegate it to. I'm not
exactly sure, but whatever reason, the one area of
conflict is that I feel that he doesn't see enough of the
kids. . . . He always has a good time with them, but
it's not enough. . . . It's more for them, too. . . .
They are never going to be this young again, this is the
time when they think back to their childhood. Are they
going to think Daddy was never there? Or are they
going to think Daddy was there? And that is what I am
concerned about. . . . He was very active in the Barris-
ters Club, and he wanted to join a men's club and do
some singing. . . . And I said, "You do not have enough
time for that. I will not let you do it," . . . that was
the only thing really that I put my foot down about. He
just didn't have an infinite amount of time and I knew
how much time that would take. . . . He was already
being pulled in too many directions. . . .
When I wasn't working I did some work for the
Opera Guild. . . . I really enjoyed it. . . . When I
started back to work I found that I really didn't have
very much time to do anything like that. . . . It was
fun doing it. If I weren't working I'm sure I'd do a lot
of it. . . . There are things that I would like to do if
I weren't so busy. There are things I plan to do when
the kids are older. . . . I guess what I'm saying is
that I probably squeeze out more time for myself than
he does, although he does have the one evening a week

that he goes and socializes. He really works so hard,
and he comes home late, and he always has work when
he comes home, and he does it after supper, and if he
doesn't do it he gets mad about not doing it. And he
plays the piano. He would love to have more time to
play the piano. He would love to have more time to
do things with the kids.

Has he considered reducing his work load?

I don't think so . . . no, I don't think he would want to
do it. And that's fine with me . . . I think because he
has a concept of his job that includes working at it full
time. . . . I don't want to give the impression that he
is one of these terrible corporate executives away on
business all the time and never has any time for his
children, because he does. And he makes a real effort
to be home so we all can have dinner together, and he
has some time for the kids after dinner.

The family attended a family camp last summer that is sponsored by the city of San Francisco. Their plan for this summer is
to attend the Lair of the Bear, a family camp sponsored by the University of California alumni.

I had a hard time getting [her husband] up there last
year, but I think he enjoyed it. This summer his firm
is scheduled for its first annual retreat one of the weekends of the week that we are gone, so we are going to
have to leave early. He does not feel that he can miss
the first one. And he arrived late last time, I forget
what the reason was, but there was some reason. So
I drove up there with the kids and he came the next day.

This pattern, in its general conformation, and the cultural expectations that are part of the pattern are applicable to roughly half
of the study's participants. The pattern includes a woman, well educated, with a considerable amount of achievement in her career; an
equally well educated and successful husband; one or two very young
children. The wife has reduced her work time but continues to ex-
pend enormous energy on her career, often attempting to carry a
full-time work load on a reduced time base. At the same time she
attempts to carry out all the role expectations of the single-career
wife. She accepts with little complaint her husband's role as a
single-career husband. There is a match between her cultural expectations and those of both the society and the organization.

The Innovators

The adapters are consistently women whose cultural expectations most closely resemble those of wives in single-career marriages, despite their own high level of career achievement. The innovators, for the most part, are much more like the people in the dual-career model—whether or not they have children.

Lynda and John met while they were undergraduates at the University of California at Davis, married in their junior year, and developed a long-range plan. John left school temporarily to work and support them while Lynda finished her degree. After her graduation she began her career in state service and John returned to school to graduate. When his degree was complete, John established his own business as a general contractor; Lynda continued to work and at the same time completed a Master in Public Administration degree. Shortly after the degree was completed, John and Lynda designed and built their "dream house" on a lot that they had purchased several years earlier. When the house was completed, the next order of business was a baby. Up to this point everything went according to plan.

Lynda had by now been working for seven years. She had begun to feel the need for a more balanced lifestyle, for more time for the community and political activities that interest her, and for more time in her home and garden.

But at the time nobody, but nobody, above the clerical ranks was working part-time, and management just wouldn't even consider it. I was told just "no way"— you'd be dead in this organization if you even suggested it.

She bided her time, and when she was pregnant she asked again.

And suddenly it was O.K. Suddenly—if you're going to be a mommy, then everybody says, "Sure, that's fine."

During the pregnancy Lynda worked half time under a job-sharing arrangement. After her daughter was born, she was ambivalent about what to do next.

My plan ran out. All those years we had planned everything. And everything had happened just as we wanted it to. But now I wanted to continue with my career, and I wanted new experiences, and I wanted

> a chance for advancement, but I also wanted to con-
> tinue to work half time. . . . I really didn't want
> to return to [the agency she had left].

She extended her maternity leave, then she and John traveled
across the country in a rented motor home—with their six-month-
old daughter. She considered consulting, rather than a part-time
position, but after considerable investigation she decided that being
self-employed would be incompatible with her goals.

Eventually she returned to her job, exercising her reinstatement rights. She sought repeatedly to be transferred to a new assignment on a half-time basis, but found that there were no open-
ings for her, despite her impressive credentials.

> I was told over and over again, "Yes, we'd love to
> have you, you'd be great for this job! But we can't
> use you on a half-time basis."

Time and patience paid off for her, however, and she was
accepted for a half-time position in a new assignment.

> It wasn't work I particularly wanted to do—it was
> really pretty boring, but I had to make a change. I
> had been in the other assignment so long—and after
> a while you look like you're really going nowhere.
> And everyone said if I had this experience, I'd be
> more competitive. So I took it, and I served my
> time there.

After nearly two years in her new assignment, Lynda left on
her second maternity leave. At the time of the interview, she was
facing the same dilemma. She is reluctant to return to the old assignment but she will do so if she can't convince someone else to
try her on a half-time basis.

She is not willing to return to a full-time assignment to prove
her competence again: "I've done that! How many times do I have
to do that?" She'll continue to seek opportunities that permit her to
get what she wants and needs from a job and that also permit her the
time that she wants and needs for the other avenues of her life.

Lynda differs from Beth and the other adapters in that her decision to reduce her time is based not on a conflict between role expectations, but on a conflict between personal aspirations. While it
would be an exaggeration to assert that Lynda and John have an ideal-
type two-career marriage, they certainly match that model in a number of important aspects. Each has a high investment in a career

and looks for work that is interesting, challenging, and rewarding.
Neither cares a great deal for the traditional status symbols of
wealth or position. Each attaches a high level of importance both
to family and to leisure. While their roles are not perfectly integrated, a good deal less role segregation exists than in Beth's marriage, for instance.

> John's self-employed. And the building business has
> a lot of slack time. He's really good about sharing—
> he really enjoys the girls and he can warm a bottle or
> change a diaper as well as I can. He's one of eight
> children himself, so it's nothing new to him. . . .
> He's really just a big kid himself—the children in the
> neighborhood come to the door and say, "Can Mr.
> _____ come out and play?" . . . He loves to fish,
> and I don't really like to do that. So he goes off by
> himself or with some of his men friends sometimes.
> . . . Last year they went to Alaska for a week. . . .
> He was so glad to get home!

Lynda feels disillusioned that she has been less successful
than she would like in finding half-time positions, but she will continue to pursue this course. At present she is using her energies
to try to increase the opportunities for part-time professional work,
using women's networks, political and social organizations, labor
unions, and other groups to proselytize. She stresses the need for
legislation, collective-bargaining agreements, and compensation
plans to support and encourage people like herself.

Other innovators are less self-consciously trend-setters, although no less influential. Chris, a personnel recruiter in an electronics manufacturing firm in California's silicon valley area, works
half time. Steve, her husband, works in local government and has
elected to work a 9/80 schedule: 80 hours spread over nine working
days, with a day off every other week. Since Chris works every
Friday, Steve takes his day off on Friday so that he can spend the
day with their son David, age two and one-half.

> He has Fridays off. He works the hours, it's just a
> different schedule. He and one other person where he
> works do that so they can have the extra day. He
> watches David and they do special things together,
> which is nice. . . . He'd love to have a reduced work
> week and reduced pay with it. He'd gladly have the
> time. . . . His earning power is much greater than
> mine would be currently, so that it wouldn't make sense

for us financially. . . . He's dreaming. . . . But he'd
love it. . . . He's very supportive. On Thursdays,
and on the Fridays that he's not off, he takes David [to
the sitter] and picks him up so I can go straight to work.

Chris's co-worker, Nancy, also enjoys the rewards of a dual-
career marriage. Like Chris, Nancy works half time as a personnel recruiter and has a young son (Jonathon, age three).

My husband keeps saying, "If your salary keeps going
up—and you're getting close to me—one of these days
I'll stay home." He takes Jonathon to the sitter on
the days I work. He even comes home in the middle
of the day to watch him if I have to stay late for a
special meeting and I was to have picked him up from
the sitter. He'll pick him up and keep him till I get
home, and then go back to work. He helps in the
house and he's been very supportive. In fact, it was
he that suggested that I continue to work if I wanted
to after the baby came. . . . He knows my personality and knew that I wouldn't fare very well if I was
home all the time. He said he really didn't think it
would be a good idea if I worked full time—he didn't
like the idea of having a baby and being away from it
all the time. He was very familiar with the split-
code program [half-time work] where he works, so
he said, "Why don't you do that?"

While Beth and her husband do not represent the ideal-type
single-career couple, and Lynda, Chris, and Nancy, with their
husbands, don't represent ideal-type dual-career couples, each
certainly has taken on at least the colorations of those categories.

When Nancy and Chris began sharing a position three years
ago, management agreed to their proposal—somewhat guardedly.
They were willing to try, since both women had been in the firm for
some time, and it was in the best interests of management to try to
keep them. The arrangement has been so successful that their
supervisor assigned Chris the task of writing up their experience
as a case study. This report has been printed and distributed by
the company, which has adopted a policy permitting and encouraging
job sharing in all of its installations. Their job-sharing arrangement has been described in several newspaper and magazine articles, which have brought considerable favorable publicity to the
company.

The Rebels

Both the adapter and the innovator groups are made up of married women. The rebels include not only some married women, but also two single men and one single woman. What this group has in common is that each has had a particularly difficult struggle against socially imposed expectations. Each in his or her own way has had to discard a role expectation that was unacceptable or uncomfortable. Robert, for instance, was a very successful systems analyst in a managerial position when he sought a mid-life career change at the age of 31. He has reduced his work week to two days and enrolled in graduate school. Shirley, a single woman with a successful career in state government, reduced her hours to half time with no purpose that was comprehensible to her employers or her peers. Joan is a highly privileged woman in every way, well educated, the daughter of a doctor, the wife of a very successful scientist. She has chosen to work at a highly demanding but very low-paying job in preference to playing out her role as corporate wife or suburban matron. Both Inez and Sarah have had to cope with ethnic expectations of them as women, wives, and mothers.

Each of them has rebelled against these expectations at a price, but each also views the rewards as sufficient. These people have achieved a match between their own expectations and their roles.

Robert received a social science degree from one of the State University of New York (SUNY) campuses ten years ago. He began his career in computers in New Jersey, and four years ago moved to San Francisco. He made rapid progress in his career and was soon promoted to a highly responsible management position. When he decided, them, to make a total career change, he understood the risks he was taking. He carefully considered the options that were available to him, in terms of both income-producing activity and leisure pursuits. Eventually, for a variety of reasons, he decided to request a reduced work load in his present organization and pursue an advanced degree in psychology.

He was rather gratified that his request was accepted as easily as it was. He is fairly insouciant about how his changed role is perceived in the organization. His friends in the neighborhood where he lives, a section of San Francisco that houses a large concentration of artists, writers, and musicians, applaud his decision.

What about, for instance, his parents? How did they respond to this action?

I called my parents and asked them if I should go to school to study art or to study psychology. That's the choice I gave them. My mother said, "Go to

> psychology because you'll have something useful you
> can do." I said, "I've been doing something useful
> for ten years."

His decision eventually was to pursue an M.A. in clinical
psychology, although not for the reasons that appealed to his mother.

> The first time—I guess—my mother sent me a letter
> that had a page and a half of shoulds! You should do
> this, and you should do that. And then she called me
> up and wanted to know why I didn't write her back. I
> said, "Well, I didn't know how to respond to these
> pages that had all these shoulds on it." She didn't
> know what to say about it. And so then she started
> reading this book on—some book that told her never
> to say should—or something . . . but then we had
> some discussions about it. . . . I don't really re-
> member them as being disapproving or anything like
> that.

Given the cultural expectations that are put on men in our society,
Robert's parents perhaps showed remarkable restraint and understanding.

Another rebel is Shirley, a single young woman in her early
thirties who is an analyst in state service. She had found herself
feeling somewhat restless and bored with life and was considering
making a career change. When she analyzed the situation more
carefully, however, she realized that the problem was not really
her job, which she liked very much, but the lack of time to pursue
her other interests—and the lack of time for herself. She began to
think of reducing her hours.

It took most of a year before she felt financially ready to make
the change, and when she did the request was greeted with absolute
astonishment by her colleagues.

> They thought of me as a "total career person," and a
> career person does not work half time.

Part of the concern of her co-workers was financial—how
could a single person live on a half salary? The more puzzling concern, to her, was the total lack of understanding of her motives.

> People kept asking me what I was going to do with my
> time—it was like, if I weren't married I wouldn't have
> anything else in my life. . . . I've always been very

active in sports, and I really missed it when I was
working full time. This last summer I've done a lot
of swimming and water skiing. . . . Last winter I
went skiing mid-week; it's great—no lines. . . . I
love to bowl; I've joined a bowling league.

In addition to these activities, she is now pursuing some community activities that were impossible on a full-time schedule.

I'm doing volunteer work at the Women's Resource
Center—career counseling for re-entry women. . . .
I'm not really involved with the women's movement,
but I do like to help women. I've got some skills that
aren't used on this job—I'm a good listener—and I have
some training in that area. . . . Before I went on half
time I was doing volunteer work at the United Way
every Saturday—working with retarded children. I
really loved it—I like the idea of working with re-entry
women too. Those things just meet some need that I
have that my job here doesn't fill. . . . I love my
job . . . when I'm here I devote full energy to it. . . .
I do more work in eight hours two or three days a week
than a lot of others do who work five days—I know, I've
worked 40 hours—I know how much you can do. . . .
I put out when I'm here, and when I go home I'm devoid
of energy. I don't have any guilt feelings. It's just
now I can also do these other things.

Some time after having switched to a reduced time base,
Shirley was married. To many of her co-workers, that explained
her "strange" choice.

It really bugged me. They immediately assumed that
that was why I had done it. Actually it has worked out
well, and I'm glad. But it disturbs me that people
were so unable to understand. . . . They just smile
and say, "Oh, so you were planning this all the time."
I wasn't, but they don't believe me.

Joan grew up in Washington State, one of three daughters of
the local physician. Over the years her father has accumulated,
piece by piece, farm land which is now worth a very large sum indeed. Her husband is a successful scientist employed in industry.
Despite her own high level of education and success, she concurred
with the social expectations of her as a mother. It has been difficult

for her to justify to herself as well as to her husband the fact that,
beyond motherhood, she needed and wanted meaningful work to do.

> We arrived in California, and four months later we had
> our first child, a son. We also agreed that it was im-
> portant that the mother be home with the children for
> the first five years. When our next child was born two
> years later, I said, "Is it five years altogether, or do
> you have to have five for each child?" I was not work-
> ing at all, but I was taking classes. I've decided, now
> that I have children and have gone through the baby
> stage, that I like children better than babies. Babies
> are too dependent. My children are now three and
> five. . . . I really enjoy them now, but I can't take
> them for extended periods of time. I could never be
> a full-time mother. I don't know if that is because I
> worked too long or because there is no esteem in
> housework. . . . Before this job came up—I had no
> way of knowing it was going to come up—I looked for a
> job. I looked where he would miss me least. So if I
> could go teach a class at night—the children would miss
> me any time—but he would be with the children. So I
> taught sewing classes at _____. . . . I am in an un-
> usual situation because Jim has a Ph.D. in nuclear en-
> gineering and he is on the staff at _____ and he will
> probably always be there. He earns a lot of money.
> There are few people who have the knowledge that he
> has in the whole world. . . . I don't have to work for
> money—but for my sanity. I have a low tolerance for
> kids. . . . So I got the job teaching classes at night,
> two nights a week, and it turned out that Jim is not
> reliable in cooking dinners, or even in caring for
> children night after night. He doesn't care if they
> have diapers on when they go to bed or not. He likes
> them on a higher plane.

Has he gained any sympathy for or understanding of her need
to have a life in addition to that of wife and mother?

> Now he has. He couldn't understand why I wanted to
> get out before, but you know what I did? I left him
> with the kids one whole day a couple of times, and he
> got the idea real quick. It has made an enormous dif-
> ference. I used to wait all day long until he came home
> and just start in like a motor mouth. And there was no

peace. And now I don't care when he gets home. He can come in and sit down and shake off the whole office routine and then voluntarily say, "Well, how was your day?"

Throughout Joan's responses several threads constantly re-appear.

> The family comes first. If the family needs anything, I'll always take time off for them.

This thread also contains a defense of her maternal instincts.

> I really love my children, I just can't take too much of them. I think I was a good mother [when they were babies] because I would go out of my way to do things for them—which is wrong. I mean—they think I am a good mother—I wait on them hand and foot.

Another thread is the need to perceive herself—validate her-self—in the larger society.

> First of all I taught a quilting class. . . . I had fun. It reminded me that I could teach, and I did enjoy it. I still see some of those students. . . . Having gotten out of just that one class—to see that I could earn my own money—I could still do something productive.

Beyond the need to prove herself as a wage earner is a need for some kind of self-expression or accomplishment.

> I belonged to the stitcher's guild, and I was really ac-tive. I would vent my frustrations on fiber, and they have an annual show and a summer project and it's not as if you weren't doing anything. . . . I have done less of that this past year—although I have this giant project in mind. . . . I never considered myself an artist. When I went into textiles it was because science was easy for me, and I like the order. It was very painful for me to take those art classes, although now that I know what teachers do—those art instructors didn't lose my assignments—the ones I really liked. I never considered myself an artist until I joined the Stitchers Guild. I never even considered creating.

Joan, happily, is able to keep her threads interwoven, literally and figuratively, because she has the gifts, not only of exceptional intelligence, but also of enormous physical energy and great
good humor. One of her supervisors commented, "If you drank
coffee, you'd be a human dynamo."

Two of the women in the group have had especially difficult
role adjustments because of ethnic expectations of them. One is
Mexican-American, the other Jewish.

Inez, a Chicana, grew up in a rural area, the youngest child
in a large, close-knit farm family. When she decided to leave home
to go to college:

> My father really didn't want me to go. He wanted me
> to go to a local [junior] college. . . . It was very,
> very hard for him. But he also knew—I'm the baby of
> the family—and he and I were very close. He also knew
> what I wanted to do. He would never have stopped me.
> He could have stopped me because there is a big hold
> there—a lot of control. . . . It was hard for him, but
> he passed away ten years ago. Before he passed away,
> he was aware of what a great opportunity I had. And
> he knew how secure I was. He was very satisfied with
> where I had gotten.

Inez's husband is from an Irish-Catholic background and now
shares with her the responsibility for their suburban home and their
two small children.

> He's great . . . when I came back to work four days a
> week, we were also in the transition of purchasing a
> new house. It was a big house. So I told him, "If I
> go back to work for four days, I'm going to need your
> help. Not only at home, but I want you to understand
> that when they're sick I can't stay home with them all
> the time. I am responsible for my job as well as you
> are for yours." I said, "if we can work out a system
> where we take turns doing the work." . . . And he's
> beautiful about that. . . . My own personal philosophy
> is that if I can't keep up the housework then I shouldn't
> work. And it is a big house—a two-story house, but
> then again the children are getting to an age where they
> can help. . . . And every now and then I will go on a
> tantrum and say, "Time out. . . . The boys clean the
> upstairs, etc.," so it works out good.

This accommodation didn't come easily, though. Chicanas generally are not taught assertiveness.

> I had to make him aware of it. . . . It took me a good
> five years to say, "Hey, you can't talk to me like that.
> I'm a human being!" And it shocked the hell out of
> him, because—I can remember the first time I couldn't
> take it any more. I remember the incident well—if I
> could freeze his face—it was such a big shock that I
> would even react like that. It was at the point where
> so much was expected of me, and I couldn't handle it.
> So I had to tell him. And he respects me and I re-
> spect him. He knows where the line is—and I know
> where it is, and we agree on that. It's a team effort.

Sarah differs from Inez in many respects. Inez and her husband live in the suburbs, send their children to day care, and do all their own gardening and housework—the gardening because they both enjoy it, the housework because she feels that it is her responsibility. Sarah and her husband live in San Francisco, employ a live-in babysitter, and in addition hire a cleaning woman and use a gardening service. Inez fully expects—and demands—equal participation in these household responsibilities from her husband. Sarah, more like Beth, protects her husband from any expectations concerning these daily concerns.

The two women are alike, however, in their struggle to overcome cultural and ethnic expectations of them as women. Inez commented:

> I feel—I went through a guilt feeling of going back to
> work and leaving my children, and the adjustments
> that they went through—and part of it—I didn't like it
> and I didn't think I could handle it. . . . I have asked
> them if they would rather that Mommy didn't work and
> they have said, "No."

Sarah requested a part-time position when her first child was born. She had to consider what she would do if her request were refused.

> My grandfather on my mother's side is from Germany.
> I used to hear some expression that he used to trans-
> late as "You never know if you don't ask"; so I have
> always been trained to ask. But, I always had to think
> about what I was going to do if the answer was not what

I wanted, and in the event that they would have said,
"No," then I would have really had to stew and think
about it, but since I got what I wanted . . . I suspect
that I would not have come back to work, because the
idea of working full time—I come from a Jewish background and there is no way, I mean the guilt trip would
have been too much! As it is I have a mother who lives
here in the city and when she finds out I have worked X
amount of hours, she says, "You're going to have problems with those children!" But she is very supportive
of me on the other hand and will pitch in if the children
need a ride and I'm not there. She herself worked part
time from the time my brother was in kindergarten,
but it was not a demanding, responsible job. She was
a fashion co-ordinator for [a specialty shop] and she
could work whatever hours she wanted. She is used to
the idea that I want time with my children and I have
often reminded her, "When we were raised, you had a
house to clean—and cook, and the laundry." I never
remember my mother being able to have a whole lot
of time for us—which we do with our children.

Sarah and the others, particularly the innovators and the
rebels, have defied the cultural expectations of them, either as
professional workers or as women and men. They have defined
their own roles and have, in the main, been successful in persuad-
ing their organizations to adapt to their roles. In that sense, every
person in the study is an innovator, and every organization involved
is, however eagerly or reluctantly, an adapter.


SOCIAL EXPECTATIONS

Social expectations concern the way in which the employee fits
into the informal fabric of the organization. On this item, there is
very little unanimity among the participants. Both the expectations
of the individuals and the degree to which the expectations are being
met vary a good deal.

One point of similarity exists. Like the middle managers
studied by Dubin and Goldman,[1] these workers do not expect to find
their central life interest in the job. The central life interest is
elsewhere, in home, family, and community, perhaps to an even
greater degree for these people than for the Dubin and Goldman
managers. They can and do respond to the organization's mandatory requirements for participation, that is, to the expectations of

the formal organization, without making the institution primary in their lives. Yet acceptance of themselves as full-scale members of the organization, with all the rights and privileges appertaining thereto, is important. Important also, but to varying degrees, are the friendships that arise in the workplace. For the most part they have found that when one changes the relationship to the formal organization, one also changes one's relationship to the informal organization.

Actually, two processes seem to occur almost simultaneously. One is that the individual begins to experience incidents that suggest that he or she is being perceived differently in the organization. The other is that the person begins to view the social structure of the organization differently.

Co-workers have a lot of ways of letting people know that their image has changed in the organization. Many people comment simply, "How did you get to do that!" or, "Boy, do I envy you!" Co-workers also subject the individuals to a lot of kidding and teasing about their choices and their options. The kidding seems to reflect several underlying attitudes; for example, that the person is no longer carrying full responsibility in the organization, or that the person is not carrying equal responsibility in the marriage.

The first of these attitudes is reflected in jokes about the individual's nonwork activities.

> Boy, what a beautiful tan! I bet you spent all day yesterday playing golf! What a life! Do you ever think of the rest of us back here, slaving away, while you're out on the golf course?

The second attitude is reflected in jokes and jibes about occurrences in the person's absence.

> I really had to cover for you yesterday—all hell broke loose. You better take me to lunch today; you really owe me one!

The third attitude comes under the guise of mock sympathy for the mate—obviously in most cases the husband.

> Poor Joe! He has to slave away all day while you're out playing tennis. And I'll bet you're too tired to fix dinner when you get home—does he have to cook for you?

All of this, it must be emphasized, is done gently, kiddingly, and good-naturedly. The women in question recognize that mixed feelings may lie behind the kidding—both some admiration and some envy. There is the recognition that there is privilege involved here. First, in order to be able to reduce working hours, one must have the agreement of management, and that agreement is usually granted only for highly valued employees. Second, one must be able to afford the reduction in pay, which suggests either a spouse with a good salary and/or good financial management. If others in the organization feel both admiration and envy, it's not too surprising. It's an enviable position!

There is a subtle difference here, however, between how co-workers perceive the adapters and how they perceive the innovators or the rebels. The adapters have a socially acceptable reason for having made this trade-off. They are, after all, sacrificing their career ambitions in order to spend time with their children. They are combining successfully two sets of cultural expectations. The innovators and the rebels, on the other hand, are making a greater departure from societal norms, in some cases rejecting those norms altogether. It is often much harder for the organization's members to understand and accept these choices, and the feeling of estrangement goes deeper.

The other side of this response from members of the organization is the change in perception that some of the people in the study have experienced toward their co-workers. As their own role choices and role definitions have changed, they tend to see others in the organization differently. They often speak in metaphors to describe the changes in their attitudes: "I seem to wear a different set of lenses these days," or, "Now when I go to work I have to sort of take off one mask and put on another one." One of the subjects who is most articulate on this notion had obviously given it a great deal of thought, and yet she still struggled to find the words to express her insights.

> This is a very sensitive area which I have to—I don't know whether I would want you to write about this but I don't mind talking about it. Since I changed my hours, I have a completely different set of what I would call, maybe, "ways of looking at the world" than I would in a work situation. And that differentiation is quite dramatic. I mean—what that means is—the way that I deal with people at work becomes kind of—it's a step back, it's less _real_. When you're not there 40 hours a week you're not a—your identity is no longer, "I am a such and such—I am a manager; I am an analyst; I am a programmer." What happens is that you no longer recognize those categories, whereas everybody that's

there has that sort of role identification. . . . Socio-
logically it's something similar to the way you approach
psychotherapy because—when you come into psycho-
therapy a person is putting—projecting—onto you different kinds of roles, like "You are like my father," "You
are like my mother," . . . and your reaction to that is
making them understand that. In the work situation you
don't necessarily want to react to the projection, but
you want to understand what projection they are making
and then deal with that in some way. The same kind of
work goes on in both areas, which is kind of interesting
to see, but it's taken me a while to get a perspective on
it, you know, to see that. . . . That's a very difficult
process, and if anybody's working part time I would
think that would be a major consideration. . . . I think
there's a sort of level of conscious understanding that
has to go on.

This switching back and forth of roles causes some role
strain and sometimes increases the difficulties of communication
with others in the organization.

If I go in and talk to my boss at work, all of the communication that goes on between us has meaning to him
and it has meaning to me, in terms of what my responsibilities are. And when he wants something done and I
have to know whether that's possible to do or not, and
yet my way of communicating with him is completely
different than from communication with somebody outside of that area . . . and so it's—you sort of become
a multifaceted person in some ways . . . and yet, all
that communication has to be real. It can't be just—
like—I'm wearing this mask today or . . . so that's
the most difficult aspect of it—but in a way it's very
liberating.

How an employee responds to these nuances varies greatly with the
individual. It may also be related to the amount of time the person
is away from the organization, to how the nonwork time is spent,
and, very much, to the employee's own personality.

Bruce, an environmental planner in California state government, has experienced some loss of status in the organization and
seems supremely unconcerned. He works only half time, his leisure is rich, and his social relationships at work have never been
significant.

    I had always felt very much like a lone wolf—like I'm
only temporary. And I've been here for years! I've
been here since 1969—but I still feel temporary. I
have never felt a part of any organization that I've
been in. I'm not a "joiner"—now there's a personality quirk that has some bearing on this, I think.

    In spite of being a "lone wolf," Bruce has always enjoyed a
good reputation in his organization. He now works every other week
and sometimes when he returns on a Monday morning he feels

    a little out of the organization—like being on a field
trip, only more so.

What is affected, however, is not his work but his social status or
his esteem in the eyes of the other men in the organization.

    In a couple of the engineering areas—they happen to be
really busy right now—there was some "What are you
doing? . . ." And then I got this sort of dark look,
like, "My gawd, I really thought better of you." What's
different is the camaraderie—the water-cooler stuff,
being one of the boys. . . . But that doesn't bother me
a bit.

    Carol, like Bruce, has never felt herself to be integrated into
the informal structure of the organization, but for her it's a bit
troublesome. Her problem is compounded by the fact that she is
both the only part-time employee in the organization and the only
woman who is married and has children. An associate editor in a
publishing house, she now works six hours a day and is the most
senior person in her division. She usually skips lunch and uses the
hour to make phone calls to the East Coast; the lines are free then
and people in New York are often in their offices at the end of the day.

    I am one of the few married people here with children
and with a husband who has an important position with
his company. He needs my support in some ways, so
that involves having big discussions. So I fall into a
hard category. I don't have any friends here . . . and
that's O.K.—but none of the others, none on the editorial side, anyway, are married women. None of
them has children . . . they are younger. There were
two women—one was older—she was very capable. She
worked at Better Homes and Gardens for years and just

wanted to move to California. She's a single person
and she doesn't have a man and she travels a lot.
There was a woman here who did have children who
were in their late teens, and she was divorced. She
and I at least had some things in common. But now
there's no one to understand that sometimes my kids
will just . . . it's disruptive and I can't help it. . . .
If I were to work full time I would never be associated
with being a wife and mother so much as they do now—
with the fact that I come later and go home earlier—
because there are plenty of things that I need to do.
. . . I frankly don't know how other women do it.
There are a few who work—on the business side—who
are married and have children, but there are not very
many—just a couple of them; I know that they are just
absolutely exhausted. I just don't want it to be that
way. It's not worth it to me.

Carol, like Bruce, has a rich and full life away from work.
She is actively involved, not only in her family and home, but also
in community activities that are very important to her. Yet, unlike Bruce, she misses the friendship and companionship of her
co-workers.

Margaret, a half-time manager, also spoke with some longing
of her lack of social interactions at work. Unlike Carol, however,
her nonwork time also keeps her from rewarding friendships. In
her case, she has opted to reduce her time because she has two
small children, and nonwork days are spent with the children.

I've really cut myself off from friends since I cut my
schedule. I like to accomplish. I appreciate my work
week, so I put out more. It's self-imposed—no one
has said, "Don't take breaks," or, "Eat your lunch at
your desk." I have lunch about once a month with a
friend here. . . . I've never been to her home, although I've been invited many times.

Janice (a manager on four-fifths time) uses her Fridays to
swim, lie in the sun, visit with her women friends—and mostly to
have time to herself. As Bruce suggests, that may be an important
variable. Both Bruce and Janice need and enjoy solitude—time to
themselves. For that reason, perhaps, social interactions at work
are enjoyable but not essential to them. For others, like Carol and
Margaret, sociability and a sense of belonging are valued, at work
as well as in leisure, and their absence causes, at the very least, a
twinge of regret.

Some people, fortunately, have been able to match their expectations. Inez, for instance, has been with the same company for 12 years. For the last six years she has served as office manager, working four days a week. She and her husband have two young children; they have a wide circle of friends as well as a large extended family; they are both very active in their church. Last year Inez served as chairperson for the school PTA fair; she is proud of the fact that they raised the largest amount of money in the history of the school. Yet she finds the time and energy to have close friendships with her co-workers.

> Yes, that is the beauty of this [company] crew. The
> people out in the warehouse are more permanent than
> in here. There is a lot of turnover here—people get-
> ting promotions—the average stay here is three years.
> So, in 1969, I was married—these people came to my
> wedding. Then my pregnancy—they catered to me,
> pampered me. They went through my father's death
> with me—which was a very hard time for me. They
> were just so nice. . . . It is just like a family—it
> really is! I feel very comfortable in sharing my life
> with them. I've gotten pretty close to a lot of these
> people. It is kind of nice because in those 12 years
> people who have left [the company] or people who
> have been promoted and are driving by will stop and
> say, "Hi." So it's a nice feeling—the people I used
> to work with, the lady that took disability—we still
> communicate. I will go see her during lunch. The
> office manager at another plant has had my husband
> and me over for lunch or whatever—it is just a friend-
> ship that you build and hold on to because they are
> really good people. . . . I am envied by so many
> people, within our family and within our circle of
> friends—because they are aware I can come and go,
> but that I don't do it, I don't abuse it. Everybody
> knows that I don't abuse it—so that is important that
> they know that.

## SUMMARY

If any conclusion can be drawn about the nature of the individuals who choose to trade time for income, it would be their uniqueness. Although Chapter 5 cites a number of points of demographic similarity, and Chapter 6 finds considerable congruency in terms of their relationship to their formal organizations, the present chapter demonstrates, in contrast, their infinite variety.

The majority of them are young, white, Protestant, well educated, and middle-class—and hence they have been exposed to very similar socialization processes—but that same assertion can also be made of the vast majority of their peers. Each of these people has chosen to change or reject, in whole or in part, some of the cultural expectations of them and to forge new relationships with the organization (both formal and informal), with family, and with the larger society. For some, this adaptation has come relatively painlessly; for others it has taken a toll.

Some view their present work schedule as ideal, while some have not yet found the combination that works best for them or their employers. Some view their present schedule either as permanent or as a step toward further reduction of work time; others look on it as temporary and plan to return to full-time work. For some, the choice has been whether to work part time or full time; for others the choice has been whether to work part time or to leave the labor force altogether. For some, the reduced schedule has provided much valued leisure and enjoyment; for others it has actually increased stress, as they attempt to meet all the expectations placed on them in their multiple roles—corporate executive, corporate wife, middle-class mother.

Whatever the motives of these individuals, one consequence of their decision (and that consequence may be intended or otherwise) is that they are serving as role models for others. Their numbers are increasing—gradually to be sure, but with gathering momentum. As they continue to demonstrate that it is possible to be a productive, contributing, and committed member of an organization, to limit the amount of time that is committed to that endeavor, to live satisfactorily—even comfortably—on a reduced income, and to enjoy the benefits that come with additional nonwork time, inevitably others begin the process of replication. Consciously or unconsciously, these people are experimental subjects; they are searching for, proposing, and testing solutions to the many problems that face contemporary organizations in responding to the needs and expectations of workers in a time of rapid and dramatic social change.

NOTE

1. Robert Dubin and Daniel Goldman, "Central Life Interests of American Middle Managers and Specialists," Journal of Vocational Behavior 2 (1972):133–41.

# 8

## MANAGERIAL CONCERNS

There is only one condition on which we can imagine
managers not needing subordinates, and masters not
needing slaves. This condition would be that each
[inanimate] instrument could do its own work, at the
word of command or by intelligent anticipation. . . .
As a shuttle should weave of itself, and a plectrum
should do its own harp playing.

Aristotle

In Chapters 5, 6, and 7, the decision of a group of professional
and managerial employees to exchange income for time was analyzed
in detail. Half of these employees work in California state service,
where a formal policy permitting voluntary reduced work-time options has recently been authorized by the state legislature. The
other half work in private-sector organizations, most of which
have no such policy. (Some have a part-time employment policy,
however.)

This chapter attempts to analyze the issue from a managerial
perspective. It attempts to look at some of the costs, benefits, and
unintended consequences that management might incur if a decision
were made to adopt a formal reduced work-time policy.

The information and the conclusions in this chapter are culled
from several sources. Much of the material is derived from the
same interviews that form the basis of the preceding chapters. In
addition, a number of secondary sources have been included: case
studies, experimental and demonstration projects, and ongoing
projects for which no formal evaluation has been undertaken. One
extensive survey of part-time employment in the private sector
also provides useful data.

All of these sources are subject to certain threats to validity and reliability. All of the case studies or demonstration projects and the survey were concerned with job sharing or permanent part-time work, rather than voluntary reduced work-time programs. All of them were limited to options of shorter work weeks. Many of the participants in the present study also were treated as part-time employees by their organizations. Two local governments in California, San Mateo County and Santa Clara County, have adopted and implemented voluntary reduced work-time programs, but no systematic research data have been collected.

Several job-sharing or permanent part-time demonstration projects have included a research component, but since different methodologies were used, cross-experiment comparison is difficult. Measures of productivity in these studies, with only one exception, are the reports of the individuals themselves, plus the subjective reports of their supervisors and peers. In only one experimental program did the nature of the work lend itself to quantification, and even in that case, as we shall see, the absence of a control group renders the findings questionable.

All of these caveats notwithstanding, a review of the available data provides some insights into the costs and benefits that management can expect.


SOURCES

Two organizations, Catalyst[1] in New York City, and New Ways to Work[2] in San Francisco, have been in the forefront of promulgating information about both job sharing and permanent part-time jobs, particularly for women with professional and managerial skills. Each is a private not-for-profit organization; each has provided consulting and advising services to women seeking career opportunities at a reduced work load; and each has also consulted with employers in implementing job-sharing and permanent part-time policies and programs. Each has accumulated and published case studies of successful job-sharing and permanent part-time experiences.

The National Council on Alternative Working Patterns, in Washington, D.C., has been active in collecting and making available information about the broad range of alternative working patterns. The council has published a directory of organizations, both public and private, that have adopted or experimented with any such alternative.[3] The Work in America Institute also has been active in promoting the idea of alternative work patterns.

Several experimental and demonstration projects on job sharing and permanent part-time work have been conducted in public-sector organizations. One of the earliest and most ambitious was undertaken in the late 1960s in the Department of Health, Education, and Welfare (HEW), then under the aegis of Secretary John Gardner.[4] The project, titled the Professional and Executive Corps, got under way in December 1967. Sixty professional and technical positions were identified as possible part-time positions, but initially only 22 of the positions were filled with part-time people. At the peak of the program only 40 women were involved. In May 1969 the first evaluation of the program was completed. A follow-up study was conducted in 1972. Although both studies found the program to be highly successful, it was allowed to dissolve after Gardner left the agency.

At about the same time that the Professional and Executive Corps project was going on in Washington, D.C., Catalyst conceived the idea of recruiting and training mature, married women college graduates as half-time social workers.[5] With support and encouragement from the Department of Health, Education, and Welfare, plus financial support from a private foundation, they eventually were able to persuade the Boston branch of the Massachusetts Department of Public Welfare to undertake the project. Fifty women participated in the research phase of the project, which lasted for two years. Two academic researchers conducted the evaluation portion of the project.

In 1974, the city of Palo Alto, California, decided to pursue the idea of job sharing in city government.[6] With technical and moral support from New Ways to Work, they committed themselves to converting 1 percent of the city's work force, eight positions, to job sharing by June 1975. The program began with two shared positions, an animal control officer and a naturalist. A third position, general librarian, was added in March 1975. All six participants were women. Although the city did not reach its 1 percent goal by the appointed time, other positions have since been converted to job sharing. Evaluation of the project was conducted by the Action Research Liaison Office at Stanford University.

In the late 1970s, the State of California carried out two demonstration projects. One was the Shared Position Project,[7] funded jointly by the Intergovernmental Personnel Act (IPA) and the State Personnel Board; the other was the Part-time Employment Pilot Project,[8] funded by the state legislature and conducted in the State Department of Motor Vehicles.

The Shared Position Project proposed to identify 30 positions in several departments that lent themselves to job sharing, to assist

the departments in filling those positions, and to monitor and eval-
uate the program.  Twenty-seven and two-fifths positions were
filled, 19 of them in clerical classes.  The evaluation research was
conducted by staff members at the State Personnel Board.

The Part-time Employment Program was a considerably more
ambitious project.  It was mandated by the legislature  in 1976 and
money was allocated for its implementation and evaluation (S.B.
570-Rains).  Unlike the Shared Position Project, the Catalyst
project, or the Palo Alto project, it did not require that employees
work half time or that they share a position with another employee.
Employees could reduce their time bases in increments of either
one-eighth or one-fifth; supervisors could hire additional part-time
employees to fill any unspent portion of their personnel allocations.
Initially, 150 positions were identified as part-time positions.  At
the time the final report was submitted in January 1979, 331 people
were participating in the program, with schedules varying from
1/5 (one day a week) to 4/5 (four days a week).  Only 5 percent
chose to work less than half time, probably because that is the cut-
off point for participation in retirement and health-insurance benefits; 40 percent worked half time; and the remainder chose a variety
of schedules.  This organization has an unusually large proportion
of clerical workers, and the vast majority of participants in the
pilot study were clerical workers.  Only nine were in technical or
professional classes.  The organization also has a largely female
work force (69 percent) and, also not surprisingly, 97 percent of
the participants were female.  The evaluation research for the pilot
study was conducted by the department's research staff.

Another very ambitious study of job sharing was undertaken
by the State of Wisconsin.  Project Join (Job Options and Innovations)
was a two-and-a-half-year experiment with job-sharing opportunities for professional and paraprofessional employees.[9]  The project
was completed in June 1979.  It was designed to include 25 positions
(50 job sharers), but actually covered 56 positions and 112 job
holders.  The participants came from a very wide range of occupations, worked in a number of departments, and utilized several
alternative scheduling possibilities, although all worked half time.
Seventy-six percent of the participants were female.  Their average
number of years of education was 16; they had, on the average, 11
years of experience.  The research component of the project was
conducted by the University of Wisconsin Department of Economics.
Funding came from the Employment and Training Administration,
U.S. Department of Labor.

The most significant piece of research on this topic that
studied private-sector firms was a survey conducted by Stanley
Nollen, Brenda Eddy, and Virginia Martin.  They were interested

in exploring how management decides to use, or not to use, permanent part-time employees, what benefits and costs are associated with using permanent part-time employees, and what work settings are or are not suited to part-time employment. To pursue these questions, they surveyed 69 firms; 39 of these were users of part-time employees and 29 were nonusers. They concentrated on two industries: manufacturing, which is the smallest user of part-time employees, and finance and insurance, which is one of the largest users. The research project was supported by the Employment and Training Administration, U.S. Department of Labor. Their book, Permanent Part-time Employment: The Manager's Perspective, also includes a helpful summary of the limited research on the topic.[10]

Four employers in California, two private-sector and two public-sector, have implemented some form of voluntary reduced work-time options without, however, including an evaluation component. These include two airlines, which have instituted a form of job sharing for flight attendants as an alternative to a lay-off, and two local governments that have instituted a voluntary reduced work-time option, partly as a budget-cutting program but also as an employee benefit.

The two airline programs are similar. The first one, at one of the largest domestic carriers, began in April 1980.[11] The company anticipated a reduction in force of 250 flight attendants. Although the union contract had no work-sharing clause, the company and the union worked out together a "partnership time off" program and developed the criteria by which the plan would be implemented.

In order to participate, flight attendants must have eight years of seniority. Any two attendants who qualify may form a partnership and be treated as one employee by the company, with the exception that each member retains her own seniority and receives full fringe benefits. The partners bid for flights using the seniority status of the senior member of the pair. They may divide the actual flights and the pay (at the rate of the senior partner) in whatever way they choose. The partners notify the company at the beginning of each month the terms of their contract, that is, how they will divide the flying time and how they want the wages distributed.

Management and the union agreed to test this plan for five months, from April 1 to September 1, 1980. The company's review showed that considerable salary savings had been achieved, greatly reducing the number of flight attendants who had to be furloughed. The company was able to retain many younger employees who would presumably have sought employment elsewhere, had they been furloughed—an important point, considering that these employees require expensive training. Employees were well satisfied with the program and very few of the potential problems—such as missed flights and conflict between partners—had occurred. Having met their objectives with a minimum of problems, the company and the union agreed to continue the program at least for the near term.

The second of the airline flight attendants' programs has not been continued. [12] This line, an international carrier, has recently undergone a merger with a domestic carrier; some complications in integrating employees and employee benefits have resulted. Further, the company is experiencing serious financial difficulties. The reduced work-time program was proposed by the flight attendants' union, and significant numbers of employees participate. Nevertheless, management decided not to continue it but to furlough employees instead.

Two local government programs, from which some limited data are available, exist in adjoining counties in California's Silicon Valley area. Santa Clara County initiated a work-sharing plan in fiscal year (FY) 1977 when it was faced with budget cuts that would have necessitated a lay-off, particularly in the Department of Social Services. The county proposed a 6.5 percent across-the-board reduction; the labor unions opposed that proposal. Negotiation finally produced a voluntary plan that permitted employees to choose 5, 10, or 20 percent reductions. Santa Clara County was one of the few counties that did not have to lay off social workers that year. In all, 1,500 county employees, out of the work force of 10,000, participated in the program. The following year, although the budget pressures had eased, employees requested that the program continue. [13] At present the employees have the option of choosing 2.5, 5, 10, or 20 percent reductions in pay and hours. They may take the time in either shorter work days or shorter work years, including occasional scheduled days off, and they contract for six-month periods. [14]

Neighboring San Mateo County, which had not avoided a lay-off in FY 1977, adopted its reduced work-hours program the following year. [15] The County Board of Supervisors has renewed the program each succeeding year. The program is very similar to Santa Clara's, except that employees choose from 5, 10, and 20 percent options and contract for a full year at a time. Participating employees receive full employee benefits and full seniority. [16] The program enjoys the full support of the labor union, with the proviso that the work load be reduced proportionately to the decrease in time and pay.

These four programs are alike in several respects: each was initiated because of an impending lay-off; each was worked out in detail with the appropriate union (or unions); and each is a voluntary program. In each case the employees maintain full seniority and benefits. Also, the employees contract with management to participate for a specific and relatively short period of time.

An important difference between these programs is the amount of time-income trade-off involved. The airline programs are variations of job sharing, requiring a one-on-one sharing between partners. The local government programs offer much greater flexibility to the employee in terms of the amount and form of the time off, but they are limited to a maximum of a 20 percent reduction, and the time must be used during the contract period; that is, it cannot be "banked" for future use.

The Federal Employees Part-time Career Employment Act of 1978 was enacted by Congress on the grounds that "part-time work may be appropriate for older workers as a transition into retirement, handicapped individuals, or others who require a reduced work week, parents who seek . . . opportunities to balance family responsibilities with the need for additional income, and students."[17] Clearly, Congress scarcely considered the possibility of reduced work time for healthy adult males.

The law defines part-time work as 16 to 32 hours a week. It requires agencies in the federal government to develop a plan to implement the law in grades GS-1 through GS-15 and to publish its plan in the Federal Register. Agencies are also required to report their progress to the Office of Personnel Management, (OPM), which is responsible for advising and assisting them in implementation of the law and also for conducting research and demonstration projects.

One deterrent to increasing part-time work in the federal government was the way that employment ceilings had been established. Before the enactment of the part-time law, ceilings were established by creating two categories—"full-time permanent" and "total." The difference between them was the "derived" ceiling and included everyone who was not permanent; employees in the "derived" category were counted on the same basis regardless of the number of hours or days that they worked. The law required that, beginning in FY 1981, agencies count permanent part-time employees on a fractional basis against their year-end personnel ceilings. Beginning in FY 1982, however, this system will be replaced by a full-time equivalent/work year (FTE) system, which means that agencies account for hours rather than for positions.[18]

Testing of the FTE system began in FY 1979 with five agencies and was expanded to ten agencies in FY 1981. Before the tests were complete, however, the Office of Management and Budget expanded the method on a government-wide basis beginning in FY 1982. Preliminary reports from the experimental agencies indicate that FTE helps to expand the use of part-time employment.

In attempting to implement the requirements of the act, some agencies have reported difficulty in recruiting or keeping part-time employees. Some agencies have expressed their view that there are insufficient numbers of true part-time candidates, but OPM staff members hypothesize that the major problem is that the traditional applicant-supply system doesn't provide the right kind of applicant. To test their hypothesis, they have undertaken a two-year experimental part-time direct-hire program.[19] In order to separate true part-time candidates, participating agencies are prohibited from converting employees hired under this program to a full-time schedule for at least one year. Transfer or reinstatement eligibility is also limited until the completion of at least one year of service. Participating agencies will report their results to OPM at the completion of the program in mid 1982.

The foregoing list of studies and programs is not intended to be exhaustive. Many other organizations, both public- and private-sector, have adopted some form of reduced work-time, job-sharing, or permanent part-time policy. Some contain a research component; more do not. The following propositions are drawn from these sources and attempt to answer as fully as possible the issues raised by managers considering whether to design and implement a voluntary reduced work-time program.

COSTS AND BENEFITS

Additional costs incurred and benefits derived will be a function of the type of policy or program adopted. For the sake of generalization, certain assumptions are necessary here. We will assume that management is considering a voluntary reduced work-time program, one in which all permanent employees in the organization have a right to request the opportunity to trade some portion of current income for some additional nonwork time, in the form of shorter work days, work weeks, or work years. We will assume that management is considering this decision for one of three reasons: to increase productivity; to avoid a lay-off; or to respond to employee demand (to present an entitlement).

Costs

Additional costs are incurred as additional employees are hired to replace lost productive capacity. The essence of the leisure-sharing proposals is that new jobs will be created in this way, providing a source of relief to secular unemployment. So

far, however, job creation has not been the purpose in experimenting or innovating, and it has not been a major unintended consequence.

In all of the cases studied so far, the purpose of the program
has been one of the three listed above. Lost productivity has been
recovered in one of several ways:

1. The job has been restructured or redesigned to improve
the productivity of the job holder.

2. The work load has been reduced.

3. Other employees have been rotated on training and development assignments.

4. Job-sharing arrangements have been implemented, either
through a new hire or by transfer.

5. Student interns have been assigned.

Only in the last two cases will additional employees be required and additional expenses be incurred. The single largest
category of increased expenses will be fringe benefits. These expenses can be divided into three categories: mandatory payroll
taxes, voluntary welfare protections, and voluntary pay-for-time-
not-worked (sometimes called compensatory) benefits.

Mandatory payroll taxes include Social Security, unemployment insurance, and workmen's compensation. Social Security
taxes are based on the employee's income. Congress establishes
both a contribution rate and a ceiling, each of which has increased
dramatically in recent years. The contribution rate through FY 1981
was 6.65 percent of the first $29,700 of income, or a total of
$1,975.05. At present the contribution rate for the years 1982,
1983, and 1984 has been set at 6.7 percent, but the salary limitations have not been enacted. [20]

If an employee reduces his or her pay and the salary is below
the Social Security ceiling, the employer's liability for Social
Security benefits will decrease. Additional Social Security tax
liability will be incurred only when the reduction in time requires
the hiring of additional employees and the pay for the job exceeds
the ceiling.

Let's take an example under the fiscal 1981 amounts. Assume
that each of five employees earns $36,000 per year. Their com-
bined payroll will amount to $180,000 and their employer will pay
$9,875.25 in Social Security taxes for them. If each one decides to
reduce job time and salary by one-sixth and take a two-month leave,
the salary is reduced to $30,000, but the Social Security tax remains
the same. If the employer then hires a sixth employee to work ten
months, and pays that employee $30,000, then an additional tax
liability of $1,975.05 occurs.

This additional cost is incurred, however, only if the salaries exceed the ceiling. Let's take another example. Five employees, each earning $24,000, decide to rotate the job and each take two months off. The employer, again, hires a replacement. At $24,000, each employee incurs for the employer an obligation of $1,608. When the salary drops to $20,000, the Social Security tax drops to $1,340. When a sixth person is hired at $20,000, the Social Security tax is also $1,340. In this case, the employer's obligation remains the same.

Here's how the arithmetic for the two examples looks:

Over the Social Security ceiling:
5 x $36,000   = $180,000          6 x $30,000   = $180,000
5 x $1,975.05 =   $9,875.25       6 x $1,975.05 = $11,850.30

Added cost = $1,975.05

Under the Social Security ceiling:
5 x $24,000 = $120,000            6 x $20,000 = $120,000
5 x $1,608  = $8,040              6 x $1,340  = $8,040

Added Social Security cost = $0

Unemployment insurance taxes work in a similar way. The employer pays a tax on all earnings up to a given ceiling. The rates are a combination of federal and state tax; the ceilings are determined by each state. [21] Individual employers' rates are adjusted according to their experience ratings; ceilings and minimum tax rates are determined by economic conditions. Because the ceilings are lower than for Social Security, additional tax would be incurred for added employees at a lower salary. However, the aggregate financial effect might be less than would occur if a layoff forced employees to claim unemployment benefits.

The third mandated expense is workmen's compensation insurance. Rates will vary widely, based upon the legal requirements and the employer's claims experience. Generally, the additional cost of workmen's compensation would be negligible.

Discretionary fringe benefits are such programs as health insurance, life insurance, dental insurance, and pension or profit-sharing programs. In California state service and in the two county programs, all employees who regularly work more than 50 percent of full time are members of the Public Employees Retirement System, which means that they are eligible not only for retirement benefits but also for employer-paid health insurance. Health insurance was also fully paid by the State of Wisconsin for the Catalyst social workers (at 90 percent of the full premium, the rate paid for all state employees). [22] Where job-sharing or voluntary reduced

work-time options have been undertaken with labor-union cooperation, full health benefits have always been sustained. The incre-
mental cost of health insurance for a newly hired employee is a
function of the number of employees in the plan and the extent of
the coverage. In very large organizations, the administrative cost
of prorating health insurance would outweigh any cash savings.
When the cost of health insurance is not prorated, it becomes a
fixed cost that is proportionately higher, since it is applied to a
lower salary base. [23]

Contributions to pension or profit-sharing plans are, like
payroll taxes, usually made on a per capita basis. The employer's
cost goes down when an employee reduces his or her income, up
when new employees are added. Employers usually cover employees in reduced work-time programs for retirement and profit sharing if they work at least 50 percent of full time, a formula generally
in accord with the provisions of Employment Retirement Income
Security Act (ERISA) of 1974. [24]

Voluntary pay-for-time-not-worked benefits are among the
easiest to deal with, since they are easily prorated. In most cases
holiday pay, vacation pay, and sick leave are prorated.

Flexible fringe-benefits programs—"cafeteria plans"—have
recently been receiving revived attention by compensation managers,
for several reasons. The most significant reason may be the steady
increase in the cost of fringe benefits, which are now estimated to
be equal to one-third of the cost of salary for the average worker.
In some organizations benefits run as high as 50 percent of salary. [25]
Under standardized benefit programs, many earners receive redundant or unneeded benefits, and from their perspective, that portion of their income is going to waste. In that case the company is
also not gaining its full value from its salary dollars.

The Revenue Act of 1978 has made it possible to remove certain employee benefits from taxable income and has provided impetus to organizations to experiment with flexible compensation. A
number of very serious potential problems cause managers to proceed cautiously. These programs are complex; they require considerable expense in administration and in educating the employees
to take full advantage of them. [26] However, they also can pay off in
improved job satisfaction. One possibility for introducing voluntary
reduced work-time options without increasing fringe-benefit costs
would be to allow employees to exchange, for example, health insurance or life insurance for additional nonjob time.

In addition to potential or actual increases in fringe-benefit
costs, employers may incur some added operating costs. Once
again, the main variable is whether new employees must be hired to
replace lost productivity.

Additional employees mean added administrative costs—personnel records, payroll costs, supervisory costs. Additional space, equipment, and supplies may be necessary. Training cost may be increased if the number of employees increases. Training is also a fixed cost that will be proportionately higher; in other words, training for a half-time employee costs the same as training for a full-time employee, but returns only half as much in performance.

Benefits

In return for the potential or actual increases in costs, employers can realize some benefits, including increased productivity (or salary savings), greater job satisfaction, added flexibility, and easier recruitment.

The issue of productivity is a complex one. Every report so far has found that employees on reduced schedules are either much more productive than their full-time counterparts, or at the very least no less productive. The results are overwhelming. Yet a manager might want to look at these results cautiously.

In the Catalyst Project involving social workers in Boston, a quantitative measure of productivity showed the half-time social workers to be astonishingly more productive than the full-time workers. Using face-to-face contacts with clients as the measure, the study showed that the half-time workers had 89 percent, rather than the expected 50 percent, as many face-to-face contacts as the full-timers. [27]

The other studies lack a quantifiable measure of productivity and rely on the self-reports of the individuals. In most cases, these perceptions are confirmed by the supervisors, and very rarely does any person report a drop in productivity.

There are a number of explanations of this phenomenon. One approach has to do with the employee per se. Reduced work-time employees have more nonjob time. Personal business and phone calls can be conducted on one's own time, while for the full-time employee a certain amount of personal business must be conducted during working hours. By the same token, routine doctor and dentist appointments can be scheduled for nonjob times when the employee works a reduced schedule. Depending on the way in which the reduced work time is taken, the employee may suffer less fatigue and stress on a daily basis and bring more energy to the job. Many employees believe that they are more motivated because of the improved schedule.

Another explanation has to do with the design of the job itself. Most jobs involve some cycles and fluctuations in work flow—slack times and pressure times. The work flow is often affected by the type of interdependency with other individuals or other units in the organization. Productivity can be increased by matching the job time to the high-demand times of the job and scheduling the nonjob time around the slack periods. This scheduling may require careful analysis of the job and more careful planning than management has typically done. Several people in the present study, both supervisors and professionals, spoke of this improved planning as an unintended consequence of reduced work time.

There are, however, some threats to validity in these studies that cannot be ignored. The work of managerial and professional employees often does not lend itself easily to productivity measurement. A manager must consider both the quantity and the quality of the work being done. In many of these cases, the improved productivity may be simply a manifestation of Parkinson's Law—or its corollary: the work may have contracted to fill the time available for its completion. In other cases the quality of the work may have suffered. It is particularly difficult to assess productivity in these studies, since there is a very limited amount of data and there are no controls.

Assuming for the moment that the reports of high productivity are accurate, there are still some questions about the likelihood that those results would continue. One possible problem is a "Hawthorne effect." These people are highly visible and tend to receive a lot of attention. If reduced work time becomes an entitlement and is widely practiced, to what extent might these productivity gains be eroded?

Another threat to validity is that these employees are not in any sense typical or average. As has been stated repeatedly, they tend to be the best and the brightest—highly valued employees with an earned reputation for outstanding performance. Comparing their performance with that of average full-time employees could be misleading, indeed. In the case of the Catalyst social workers, the participants in the study were an elite group; they were educated, mature, married women from well-to-do suburban families. A very extensive publicity campaign had produced over 1,500 responses, from which 250 applications were received and the 50 participants selected. The members of the full-time group with which they were compared were younger, mostly unmarried, and working on their first job. "They were somewhat less liberal in their attitudes and less likely to take as much pride in their work than were the Catalyst women."[28] While the high level of performance is impressive indeed and supports the claim that married women represent a tremendously underutilized resource, it fails to support a claim that permitting full-time employees to reduce their work time will result in dramatic increases in productivity.

What the present study does support, overwhelmingly, is the claim that, with careful planning, workers can reduce their work weeks by as much as 20 percent and produce work equivalent in both quantity and quality. In those cases management gains both a salary savings and a satisfied employee.

If management chooses to adopt a voluntary reduced work-time program in order to increase productivity, the program will succeed if, and only if, there is a systematic analysis of the job, its technology, the cycles and fluctuations of the work flow, and the scheduling preferences of the individual. It has become fashionable in management-training circles to prefer the term effectiveness to efficiency—doing the right things rather than doing things right. Efficiency has become a pejorative term, often associated with authoritarian managers insensitive to the human needs of their employees—with production-oriented managers. There is nothing inherently wrong, though, with being efficient. Increased productivity is as likely to come from better planning and management, from improved utilization of human resources, as from improved motivation or from a higher marginal input of energy.

Employers can also expect to benefit by improved job satisfaction, however. In all of the studies, including this one, employees report a high level of satisfaction with their schedules. They tend to perceive either the organization as a whole or their unit management as innovative, progressive, and responsive to the human needs of the employees. They enjoy an increased sense of personal autonomy, more-satisfying family life, and more-rewarding leisure. Even employees who don't take advantage of the opportunity report general satisfaction with the concept and often look forward to some time at which they will participate.

Once again, one must proceed cautiously. There are potential problems and potential conflicts involved. Supervisors and colleagues may fear that the individual will exploit the situation. They may fear that the work load will be unequally divided, that the person may fail to carry his or her full share of the work load. Supervisors fear a loss of control and co-ordination. Obviously these are valid concerns. If either managers or colleagues perceive the idea as unprofessional, they may feel personally demeaned and threatened. If the privilege is awarded selectively to high achievers, other organization members may come to view it as an entitlement and become angry and disappointed if they discover it is not.

Participating employees may experience a decline in job satisfaction as well. These employees sacrifice not only pay but also both lateral and upward mobility. Some feel that the penalties are too great. Others feel that they are the exploited, not the exploiters. If they have reduced their pay and their time, but not their work load, they may end up taking work home, or coming in or staying in on nonjob time. This hazard is particularly salient when the purpose of the program is to implement salary cuts without a lay-off. Unless the level of services is also reduced and the work load adjusted, the employees are victims of a "speed-up."[29] In these cases their sense of exploitation will be supported by labor unions and professional organizations.

The employees may also experience some feelings of dissatisfaction because of the loss of social contacts in the organization, a reduction in status among their peers, or the diminished feelings of self-worth that are associated with a reduced income. For these reasons, some employees may choose to return to full-time work or may wish to experiment with some other schedule.

These potential sources of job dissatisfaction can largely be avoided by careful planning and good management. When the job is reasonably designed to meet the needs of the organization and the job holder, and when opportunities are equitably distributed within the organization, many of these potential problems will be avoided.

Increased flexibility can be a benefit to management as well as to individuals. When the work flow is cyclical or erratic, having available a pool of workers with flexible schedules makes it easier to increase or decrease strength as necessary. For nonexempt employees, this flexibility may produce a decrease in overtime pay. Additional back-up strength may be available to replace employees who are absent or on leave; additional training and development opportunities can be created by rotating employees to replace lost time and productivity. An innovative manager will find a number of ways to strengthen his or her organization through the creative application of the increased flexibility.

Employers in some industries are experiencing enormous difficulty in recruiting employees in highly skilled occupations. Many inducements are offered—high salary, moving expenses, athletic and recreational facilities, and more. One important perquisite is shorter hours, including more holiday and vacation time. Recruiters may soon find that a voluntary reduced work-time option enhances their recruiting efforts in these highly competitive occupations. Creating part-time professional and technical jobs has not seemed to attract many applicants, presumably because of all the deterrents to part-time work, but voluntary reduced work-time options may be valued by employees who would not consider a part-time job.

Critics of reduced work-time options often predict that this flexibility, rather than being a benefit, will create an administrative nightmare. Little evidence so far supports that assertion. On the contrary, the evidence so far shows that, with careful management, the benefits far outweigh the costs.

RECAPITULATION

A number of case studies, experiments, demonstration projects, and surveys are available on such allied constructs as job sharing, permanent part-time work, and reduced work hours. Although these lack methodological consistency, they provide a base of experience on which some generalized propositions can be tested.

Employers should consider voluntary reduced work-time policies for any of several reasons—to increase productivity (or achieve salary savings), to provide an alternative to a lay-off, or to respond to the needs of their employees for better balance of job, family, and leisure.

Additional payroll costs will be incurred if the program results in hiring additional employees. It may be possible to adjust benefit costs by including voluntary reduced work time as part of a flexible compensation program.

If a program is well planned and well executed, it can provide salary savings, added productivity, improved job satisfaction, increased flexibility in scheduling, and enhanced recruiting. Poor planning may lead to loss of control, lower productivity, increased conflict, and reduced job satisfaction, for both the employees participating in the program and their peers.

Organizations will need to develop carefully conceived policies and procedures to accomplish the desired results and avoid the possible pitfalls. Policies should be developed that will determine:

1. Employees' rights, responsibilities, and protections when they request a reduced schedule.
2. Supervisors' rights, responsibilities, and protections when they grant a reduced work-time request.
3. Which employees are or are not eligible to request participation.
4. The criteria to be applied in considering an employee's request.
5. The conditions under which a request might be denied or revoked.
6. The circumstances under which an employee will be permitted to withdraw from the program or modify his or her schedule.

Large organizations may wish to experiment with a limited number of options. Initially, they may also want to limit the forms in which the time can be taken, with the choices based upon the determination of the employees' preferences. As in all innovations, the total support of top management is essential, and where there is a collective-bargaining contract, the union support will also be essential. Middle managers and supervisors will need to be trained in planning and executing the program so that the desired objectives are met. The training will concentrate on efficiency, on making efficient use of the employees' on-the-job time. With careful planning and execution, voluntary reduced work-time options can provide employees with a much-valued benefit. At the same time, the organization can improve its own management practices and benefit from greater efficiency. The key is in good management.

NOTES

1. Catalyst, Flexible Work Schedules, A Catalyst Position Paper, New York, 1973.
2. New Ways to Work, Reduced Work Time Options: A Selected Bibliography, San Francisco, 1981.
3. National Council on Alternative Work Patterns, Alternative Work Schedule Directory, Washington, D.C., 1978.
4. Marjorie Silverberg and Lorraine Eyde, "Career Part-time Employment: Personnel Implications of the Department of Health, Education, and Welfare Professional and Executive Corps," Good Government (Fall 1971):11-19; cf. Margaret Howell, "Evaluating the Professional and Executive Corps of the Department of Health, Education, and Welfare," Public Personnel Management (January 1973):37-41; Marjorie Silverberg, "Part-time Careers in the Federal Government," The Bureaucrat (Fall 1972):247-51.
5. Catalyst, Part-time Social Workers in Public Welfare, New York, October 1971.
6. Cheryl Stewart, Joanne Kennedy, Christine Sierra, and Charles Gossett, Job Sharing in Municipal Government: A Case Study in the City of Palo Alto, California, Action Research Liaison Office, Stanford University, 1975.
7. Final Report on the Shared Position Project: Expanded Use of Part-time Employment, Policy and Standards Division, California State Personnel Board, July 1978, IPA Project No. 76-21.
8. The Part-time Employment Pilot Program, Report to the Governor and the Legislature of the State of California, California Department of Motor Vehicles, January 1979.
9. State of Wisconsin, Project Join Final Report (Madison, Wisc.: Department of Employment Relations, 1979).
10. Stanley Nollen, Brenda Eddy, and Virginia Martin, Permanent Part-Time Employment: The Manager's Perspective (New York: Praeger Special Studies, 1978).
11. Telephone conversations with the Assistant to the Director of In-Flight Services, July 12, 1980, and June 22, 1981.

12. Telephone conversation with International Union of Flight Attendants Office in San Francisco, July 10, 1981.

13. Testimony of Dan McCorquodale, Santa Clara County Board of Supervisors, in Leisure Sharing, hearing before the Select Committee on Investment Priorities and Objectives, California Legislature, November 1977.

14. Telephone conversation with Mabel Delong, Employee Relations Department, Santa Clara County, June 19, 1981.

15. Testimony of Linda Gregory, AFSCME business agent, in Leisure Sharing, op. cit.; and telephone conversation with Linda Gregory, June 18, 1981.

16. Telephone conversation with Michael Ray, San Mateo County Personnel Department; interdepartmental correspondence to County Board of Supervisors.

17. Federal Employees Part-time Career Employment Act of 1978 (Public Law 95-437).

18. Federal Personnel Manual System, FPM Bulletin 340-5, August 25, 1980.

19. Office of Personnel Management, Interagency Advisory Group, Experimental Part-time Hire Program, January 1980.

20. Telephone conversation with Internal Revenue Service Information Office, June 26, 1981.

21. Telephone conversation with Audit Division, California State Department of Employment Development, June 26, 1981.

22. State of Wisconsin, Project Join Final Report.

23. Nollen et al., Permanent Part-Time Employment.

24. Ibid.

25. "New Life for Flexible Compensation," Dun's Review (September 1978):66-70; cf. "New Tax Law Encourages Companies to Offer Employees 'Menu' of Benefits in Cafeteria Compensation Programs," World of Work Report (February 1979):10-11.

26. James W. Shea, "Cautions about Cafeteria-Style Benefit Plans," Personnel Journal (January 1981):37-38, 58.

27. Catalyst, Part-time Social Workers.

28. Ibid., p. 23.

29. Testimony of Linda Gregory, Leisure Sharing.

# 9

## EPILOGUE

The certainties of one age are the problems of the
next.

R. H. Tawney

The preceding pages have presented as comprehensive a picture as possible of the dynamics of the concept of voluntary reduced
work time for professional and managerial employees in complex
organizations. The time has come to try to summarize the evidence,
draw some conclusions, and speculate about the future.

The vast majority of complex organizations, certainly of the
ones represented in this study, operate under a standard work week,
a fixed schedule, and a common package of fringe benefits for their
employees. Most also have developed a more or less fixed career
path for their rising young executives, one that assumes a linear
pattern of full-time and uninterrupted work. Extant organizational
theory, which assumes a masculine work ethic and which asserts
the need for a balance between "concern for product" and "concern
for people," rarely challenges the assumptions of these rigid policies.

These standard and fixed procedures originated in an earlier
age, an industrial age, and in earlier economy, one characterized
by exchange, growth, and the availability of cheap energy and abun-
dant resources. They assume a family pattern in which the model-
class family consists of a male breadwinner with a dependent wife
and children. They have their roots in a set of social values, a
work ethic, that was consistent with that social world. They were
entirely appropriate in that era.

In the early days of the industrial era, high investment in capital equipment necessitated a steady supply of labor. Machinery

159

dictated the pace and the place of work; employees exchanged their
time for money and their money for goods. Fixed time schedules
and rates of pay were essential to assure maximum productivity.

In this exchange economy, continued economic growth was
essential but not always a reality. The extreme changes characteristic of economic cycles brought enormous hardship to unemployed workers and their families. As technology improved, productivity increased faster than demand, and hours of work were
gradually shortened to decrease the supply of labor.

The roles of men and women became greatly segregated. Men
spent very long hours in the workplace; their women and children
lived in crowded urban conditions. The men did market work; they
earned the money. Women did nonmarket work. Men were pro-
ducers; women and children were consumers. The man's wages had
to be adequate to provide not only for himself but also for the whole
family. As fringe benefits were added to wages, employers took
over responsibility for the health and welfare of both worker and
family.

With this emerging social world came the Reformation. The
relationship between Protestantism and capitalism is complex and
beyond the scope of this work. The point is that during this period
the virtues of hard work, independence, and providing for one's own
took on a sacred value. The Protestant work ethic was born. Both
organizational theory and public policy have their roots deeply em-
bedded in the values and assumptions of the traditional work ethic.

The world has changed, however. While many of these conditions and these values persist, a monolithic view of the world no
longer represents reality. For a great many workers and a great
many organizations, the postindustrial society has arrived, and with
it have come diversity and pluralism.

The electronic revolution—the semiconductor and the products
that it makes possible—has freed many workers from time and place
constraints. With a microprocessor, workers can work wherever
and whenever it is expedient to do so. Productivity is no longer a
function of the ability of a machine to produce; rather, it is a function of the ability of the employee to utilize the resources available.

While the exchange economy still predominates, a large and
growing grants economy exists. One function of the grants economy
is to reduce greatly the economic vulnerability of workers. While
economic policy continues to be predicated on assumptions of growth,
many policy makers are expressing concern about the effects of
growth on our physical and social environment. Some continue to
assert that a steady-state economy is possible and desirable.

The most significant changes are probably those that have occurred in families and in family life. Both the form and the substance

of family life have undergone enormous change. The single-career couple, headed by a breadwinner with full responsibility for providing the financial security of the household, now represents only a small fraction of American families. The two-paycheck and two-career family, with or without children, the single-person household, and the single-parent family are all present in significant numbers. These households have divergent needs for income and for health and welfare protection.

Just as the Industrial Revolution was closely related to the emergence of the Protestant work ethic, the postindustrial revolution has brought with it a whole new set of social values. While the work ethic is certainly strong and well, it has undergone significant changes, including a redefinition of the meaning of success and an increase in the value and meaning of leisure—that is, an emerging leisure ethic.

Has organizational theory kept pace? Apparently not; while organizations have made some concessions to the demands of dual-career couples, particularly those with children, there seems to be as yet very little recognition of the magnitude of the changes that have occurred or are occurring. Organizational theorists, deeply concerned about both job satisfaction and productivity, look to a variety of job redesign and quality-of-work-life interventions. They study the power relationships or the decision-making processes in the organization; they propose organizational development programs to improve the interpersonal communication and problem-solving abilities in the organization; they consider various wage incentive approaches. They increasingly frequently apply compressed work-week and flexitime plans. However, they rarely, if ever, consider releasing the organization from the rigidity of standard work hours, inflexible career paths, and uniform pay and benefit packages. Reduced work time, if it is considered at all, is considered in the form of permanent part-time work or job sharing for married women.

The study reported upon here suggests some of the creative ways in which reduced work time could be applied. It provides evidence that, in a broad sense, very little change is occurring, and that, in a more specific sense, very important changes are occurring.

Most of the employees in the survey work for very large organizations, half in California state service, the other half in private-sector firms. Only two of the private-sector firms have a policy that covers reduced work time, and management in the other firms shows no enthusiasm for creating one. All but one of the private-sector employees is female. Each one is clearly a corporate deviate, both through having a reduced schedule and through being exceptionally talented and able. In spite of these employees' success in adjusting their schedules and in maintaining their high performance,

very few of their peers seek to imitate them. Certainly their male
peers seem not to consider such a path viable for them.

In state service, however, the picture is quite different. Because of the research projects that have been conducted, because of
the role models that have been set, and because of the entitlement
contained in new legislation,* the number of employees choosing
some form of reduced work time is increasing rapidly. In some departments, it has become nearly commonplace for people to request
and be granted some form of reduced work time. In other departments, management is still very resistant.

Increasing numbers of men in state service are participating
and are expressing interest in participating. This male acceptance
is essential if the concept is to take hold. As long as only women
participate, they will always be perceived as an elite group—which
will remain what one woman called a "female ghetto." However, if
men, the mainstream of the organization, the men in line positions,
exercise their option to reduce their pay and their hours, then, and
only then, will the program be considered a legitimate option for all
professional and managerial employees. This is not to understate
the importance of the contribution of the women who have been innovators and rebels in their organizations—they are the ones who have
legitimized the concept for professional employees; but until the alternative of reduced work time is viable for all employees, these
leaders will continue to jeopardize their own standing in the organization.

The California law has one important limitation. It allows for
workers to reduce their pay with a concomitant reduction in time,
in the form of either shorter work weeks or shorter work days. It
does not include options for shorter work years, such as a 4 percent
reduction in pay for an additional ten days of vacation, or a 20 percent reduction in pay in exchange for a ten-week leave. The available evidence suggests that these options are in fact the ones that
would be most attractive to male workers. It also does not provide
the opportunity for employees to "bank" reduced work time over fiscal years and save for a sabbatical leave, parental leave, educational
leave, or early retirement. These variations would increase the administrative complexity of the program but would also increase the
organization's and the individual's flexibility. These variations may
someday be included in a flexible compensation program.

These suggestions may seem extreme, even bizarre, to some—
but not so long ago, ideas such as job sharing, flexitime, compressed
work weeks, and flexible compensation seemed equally fanciful. Not

---

*The Reduced Work Time Act of 1980 (S.B. 1859-Rains).

long before that, the idea of careers for women, especially married women with children, was considered aberrant.

During the Great Depression, the standard work week was shortened to 40 hours, a figure we have since come to think of as standard. It would be unthinkable to us to consider going back to a time when workers routinely worked 70 hours a week. Future generations may find it equally unthinkable that all workers would comply to an inflexible and unvariable schedule.

## IMPLICATIONS OF LINEAR-SEPARABLE PERCEPTION OF TIME: A FINAL WORD

Labor does not, by its very nature, fall into units of eight-hour days, five-day weeks, and 50-week years, nor do human beings, by their nature, labor most efficiently on this schedule. The standard work week was not devised from economizing or utility-maximizing principles so much as it evolved through the economic and political processes of a market-centered economy based on instrumental rationality. Jobs have been designed to fit into this predetermined work week, rather than the reverse.

There is no moral or ethical value to a five-day, 40-hour work week except that which the society has conferred on it. The length of the standard work week is not written on tablets of stone. It is a phenomenon dating back only to the late 1930s and determined not by God but by the United States Congress.

If we begin to free our thinking from the rigidity of the 40-hour week, if we begin to think in terms of scheduling jobs around the tasks themselves rather than on some arbitrary time schedule, if we begin to remove artificial constraints of time and place, then it may be possible for organizations to achieve their purposes of efficiency; for employees to achieve their need for actualization in other areas; and for the society as a whole to benefit.

# BIBLIOGRAPHY

ARTICLES AND CHAPTERS

Albee, George. "The Protestant Ethic, Sex and Psycho-Therapy."
American Psychologist 32 (February 1977):150-61.

Bane, Mary Jo. "Here to Stay: Parents and Children." In Family
in Transition, 3d ed., edited by Arlene Skolnick. Boston: Little,
Brown, 1980.

Benson, Rosen, and Thomas Jerdee. "Dual Career Marital Adjustment: Potential Effects of Discriminatory Managerial Attitudes."
Journal of Marriage and the Family (August 1975):565-72.

_____. "Sex Stereotyping in the Executive Suite." Harvard Busi-
ness Review 52 (March/April 1974):45-58.

Best, Fred. "Preferences on Worklife Scheduling and Work-Leisure
Tradeoffs." Monthly Labor Review 101 (June 1978):31-37.

Best, Fred, and Barry Stern. "Education, Work and Leisure: Must
They Come in That Order?" Monthly Labor Review 100 (July
1977):3-10.

Buckholz, Rogene. "An Empirical Study of Contemporary Beliefs
about Work in American Society." Journal of Applied Psychology
63 (April 1977):219-27.

Cooper, M. S., B. S. Morgan, P. M. Foley, and L. B. Kaplan.
"Changing Employee Values: Deepening Discontent." Harvard
Business Review 57 (January/February 1979):117-25.

Denny, Reuel. "The Leisure Society." Harvard Business Review
37 (May/June 1959):46-60.

Deuterman, William V., Jr., and Scott Campbell Brown. "Voluntary Part-Time Workers: A Growing Part of the Work Force."
Monthly Labor Review 101 (June 1978):3-10.

Dubin, Robert, and Daniel Goldman. "Central Life Interests of American Middle Managers and Specialists." Journal of Vocational Behavior 2 (1972):133-41.

Elbing, Alvor O., Herman Gadon, and John R. M. Gordon. "Flexible Working Hours: It's About Time." Harvard Business Review 52 (January/February 1974):18-34.

Etzioni, Amatai. "Opting Out: The Waning of the Work Ethic." Psychology Today, July 1977, p. 18.

Foegen, J. H. "If It Means Moving, Forget It." Personnel Journal (August 1977):414-16.

Goldston, Eli. "Executive Sabbaticals: About to Take Off?" Harvard Business Review 51 (September/October 1973):57-68.

Gordon, Nancy. "Institutional Responses: The Social Security System." In The Subtle Revolution: Women at Work, edited by Ralph E. Smith. Washington, D.C.: The Urban Institute, 1979.

Graham, Robert J. "The Role of Perception of Time in Consumer Research." Journal of Consumer Research 7, no. 4: 335-42.

Greenwald, Carol, and Judith Liss. "Part-Time Workers Can Bring Higher Productivity." Harvard Business Review 51 (September/October 1973):20+.

Grønseth, Erick. "The Breadwinner Trap." In The Future of the Family, edited by Louise Kapp Howe. New York: Simon and Schuster, 1972.

Hackman, J. P. "The Design of Work in the 1980's." Organizational Dynamics 7 (Summer 1978):3-17.

Hedges, Janice Neipert. "Flexible Schedules: Problems and Issues." Monthly Labor Review 100 (February 1977):62-64.

Hedges, Janice N., and Geoffrey H. Moore. "Trends in Labor and Leisure." Monthly Labor Review 94 (February 1971):3-11.

Howell, M. A., and M. G. Ginsburg. "Evaluation of the Professional and Executive Corps of the Department of Health, Education, and Welfare." Public Personnel Management 2 (January 1973):37-42.

Janney, Mary D. "Designing Jobs for People: Flexible Hours for Women (and Men)." Good Government 91 (Summer 1974):8-11.

Kanter, Rosabeth Moss. "Work in the New America." Daedalus 107 (Winter 1978):47-78.

Kelley, John R. "Work and Leisure: A Simplified Paradigm." Journal of Leisure Research 4 (Winter 1972):50-62.

Kidron, Aryeh. "Work Values and Organizational Climate." Academy of Management Journal 21 (June 1978):239-47.

Kotter, John Paul. "The Psychological Contract: Managing the Joining Up Process." California Management Review 15 (Spring 1973):91-99.

Leon, Carol. "The Employment-Population Ratio: Its Value in Labor Force Analysis." Monthly Labor Review 104 (February 1981):36-45.

Leon, Carol, and Robert W. Bednarzik. "A Profile of Women on Part-Time Schedules." Monthly Labor Review 101 (October 1978):3-12.

Leontief, Wassily. "Worksharing, Unemployment, and Economic Growth." In Work, Time and Employment. A special report to the National Commission for Manpower Policy, Special Report No. 28, October 1978.

Levitan, Sar, and Richard Belous. "Work-Sharing Initiatives at Home and Abroad." Monthly Labor Review 100 (September 1977): 16-20.

Locher, Alan. "Short-Time Compensation: A Viable Alternative to Layoffs." Personnel Journal (March 1981):213-16.

London, Manuel, Rich Crandall, and Gary Seals. "The Contribution of Job and Leisure Satisfaction to Quality of Life." Journal of Applied Psychology 62 (June 1977):328-33.

Mandt, Edward. "Managing the Knowledge Worker of the Future." Personnel Journal 57 (March 1978):138-43.

Martin, G. Lowell. "A View of Work Toward the Year 2000." Personnel Journal 56 (October 1977):502-04.

Martin, Virginia H. "Recruiting Women Managers Through Flexible Hours." S.A.M. Advanced Management Journal (July 1974), 46-53.

Marx, Karl. "Alienated Labor." In Man Alone: Alienation in Modern Society, edited by Eric Josephson and Mary Josephson. New York: Dell, 1965.

Maynard, Cathleen. "Mobility and the Dual-Career Family." Personnel Journal (July 1979):468-82.

Mertes, Louis. "Doing Over Your Office—Electronically." Harvard Business Review 59 (March/April):127-35.

Moore, Kristin, and Isabell Sawhill. "Implications of Women's Employment for Home and Family Life." In Women Working: Theory and Facts in Perspective, edited by Ann Stromberg and Shirley Harkess. Palo Alto, Calif.: Mayfield, 1978.

Moore, Kristin, and Sandra Hofferth. "Women and Their Children." In The Subtle Revolution: Women at Work, edited by Ralph E. Smith. Washington, D.C.: The Urban Institute, 1979.

Mooney, Marta. "Does It Matter If His Wife Works?" Personnel Administrator (January 1981):43-49.

Mills, D. Quinn. "Human Resources in the 1980s." Harvard Business Review 57 (July/August 1979):154-62.

Neulinger, John, and Miranda Brett. "Attitude Dimensions of Leisure: A Replication Study." Journal of Leisure Research 3 (Spring 1971):108-15.

"New Life for Flexible Compensation." Dun's Review (September 1978):66-70.

"New Tax Law Encourages Companies to Offer Employees 'Menu' of Benefits in Cafeteria Compensation Programs." World of Work Report (February 1979):10-11.

Noe, Francis P. "Autonomous Spheres of Leisure Activity for the Industrial Executive and Blue Collarite." Journal of Leisure Research 3 (Fall 1971):220-49.

_____. "The Political and Social Ideology of the Leisure Class." Journal of Leisure Research 5 (Summer 1973):49-59.

Nord, Walter. "Job Satisfaction Revisited." American Sociologist 32 (December 1977):1026-35.

O'Leary, James F. "Skole and Plato's Work Ethic." Journal of Leisure Research 5 (Spring 1973):49-55.

Olmsted, Barney. "Job Sharing: A New Way to Work." Personnel Journal 56 (February 1977):78-81.

Orzack, Louis. "Work as a 'Central Life Interest' of Professionals." Social Problems 7 (Fall 1959):125-32.

Owen, John D. "Why Part-Time Workers Tend to Be in Low Wage Jobs." Monthly Labor Review 101 (June 1978):11-14.

_____. "Workweeks and Leisure: An Analysis of Trends, 1948-1975." Monthly Labor Review 99 (August 1976):3-8.

Pleck, Joseph, Graham L. Staines, and Linda Long. "Conflicts between Work and Family Life." Monthly Labor Review 103 (March 1980):29-31.

Ramos, Alberto Guerreiro. "A Theory of Social Systems Delimitation." Administration and Society 8 (August 1976):249-71.

Rom, Betty L. "Part-Time Professional, Full-Time Woman." HUD Challenge (March 1971):28-30.

Rones, Phillip L. "Older Men: The Choice between Work and Retirement." Monthly Labor Review 101 (November 1978):3-10.

_____. "The Retirement Decision: A Question of Opportunity." Monthly Labor Review 103 (November 1980):14-17.

Rosenfeld, Carl, and Scott Campbell Brown. "The Labor Force Status of Older Workers." Monthly Labor Review 102 (November 1979):12-18.

Safilios-Rothschild, Constantina. "Women and Work: Policy Implications and Prospects for the Future." In Women and Work, edited by Ann Stromberg and Shirley Harkess. Palo Alto, Calif.: Mayfield, 1978.

Samuelson, Robert J. "A Rebel with Cause." National Journal, April 26, 1980.

Sawhill, Isabel V. "Economic Perspectives on the Family." In The Economics of Women and Work, edited by Alice Amsden. New York: St. Martin's Press, 1980.

Schonberger, Richard. "Inflexible Working Conditions Keep Women 'Unliberated.'" Personnel Journal 50 (November 1971):834-38.

_____. "Private Lives versus Job Demands." Human Resource Management 14 (Summer 1975):27-32.

Schrank, Robert. "Horse-Collar Blue-Collar Blues." Harvard Business Review 59 (May/June 1981):133-38.

Schwartz, Felice. "Converging Work Roles of Men and Women." Business and Society Review/Innovation 7 (Autumn 1973):71-75.

_____. "New Work Patterns: For Better Use of Woman Power." Management Review 63 (May 1974):4-12.

Shea, James. "Cautions about Cafeteria-Style Benefit Plans." Personnel Journal (January 1981):37-38, 58.

Silverberg, Marjorie M. "Part-Time Careers in the Federal Government." Bureaucrat 1 (Fall 1972):247-51.

Silverberg, Marjorie, and Lorraine Eyde. "Career Part-Time Employment: Personnel Implications of the HEW Professional and Executive Corps." Good Government 88 (Fall 1971):11-19.

Singer, James W. "Sharing Layoffs and Jobless Benefits: A New Approach Is Attracting Interest." National Journal, February 9, 1980, pp. 232-35.

Sonnenfield, Jeffrey. "Dealing with the Aging Work Force." Harvard Business Review 56 (November/December 1978):81-92.

Spreitzer, Elmer, and Eldon Snyder. "Work Orientation, Meaning of Leisure and Mental Health." Journal of Leisure Research 6 (Summer 1974):207-19.

Staines, Graham, and Pamela O'Connor. "Conflicts among Work, Leisure, and Family Roles." Monthly Labor Review 103 (August 1980):35-39.

Tilgher, Adriano. "Work through the Ages." In Man, Work and Society: A Sociology of Occupations, edited by Sigmond Nosow and William Forms. New York: Basic Books, 1962.

Tiger, Lionel. "Is This Trip Really Necessary?" Fortune, September 1974, pp. 130-41.

Vanek, Jo Ann. "Time Spent in House Work." In The Economics of Women and Work, edited by Alice H. Amsden. New York: St. Martin's Press, 1980.

Vickery, Clair. "Women's Economic Contribution to the Family." In The Subtle Revolution: Women at Work, edited by Ralph E. Smith. Washington, D.C.: The Urban Institute, 1979.

Walton, Richard E. "Work Innovations in the United States." Harvard Business Review 57 (July/August 1979):88-98.

Werther, William, Jr. "Mini-Shifts: An Alternative to Overtime." Personnel Journal 55 (March 1976):130-33.

_____. "Part-Timers: Overlooked and Undervalued." Business Horizons 18 (February 1975):13-20.

Whyte, William. "The Wives of Management." Fortune, October 1951, 86-88, 204, November 1951, 109-11, 150.

Yankelovich, Daniel. "The Meaning of Work." In The Worker and the Job: Coping with Change, edited by Jerome Rosow. Englewood Cliffs, N.J.: Prentice-Hall, 1974.

_____. "New Rules in American Life: Searching for Self-Fulfillment in a World Turned Upside Down." Psychology Today, April 1981, pp. 35-91.

_____. "Work, Values and the New Breed." In Work in America: The Decade Ahead, edited by Jerome Rosow and Clark Kerr. New York: D. Van Nostrand, 1979.


BOOKS

Amsden, Alice, ed. The Economics of Women and Work. New York: St. Martin's Press, 1980.

Anthony, P. D. The Ideology of Work. London: Tavistock Publications, 1977.

Arendt, Hannah. The Human Condition. Chicago, Ill.: University of Chicago Press, 1958.

Aristotle. Politics. Translated by Ernest Barker. London: Oxford University Press, 1972.

Bernard, Jessie. The Future of Marriage. New York: Bantam Books, 1972.

Best, Fred. Flexible Life Scheduling: Breaking the Education-Work-Retirement Lockstep. New York: Praeger, 1980.

Blauner, Robert. Alienation and Freedom: The Factory Worker and His Industry. Chicago, Ill.: University of Chicago Press, 1964.

Boulding, Kenneth. Ecodynamics. Beverly Hills: Sage, 1978.

_____. The Economy of Love and Fear. Belmont, Calif.: Wadsworth, 1972.

Boulding, Martin, and Martin Pfaff, eds. Redistribution to the Rich and the Poor. Belmont, Calif.: Wadsworth, 1972.

Burns, Scott. Home, Inc. New York: Doubleday, 1975.

Campbell, Angus, Philip E. Converse, and William L. Rodgers. The Quality of American Life: Perceptions, Evaluations and Satisfactions. New York: Russell Sage Foundation, 1976.

Cheek, Neil H., Jr., and William R. Burch. The Social Organization of Leisure in Human Society. New York: Harper & Row, 1976.

Clark, Dennis. Work and the Human Spirit. New York: Sheed and Ward, 1967.

Cohen, Allan, and Herman Gadon. Alternative Work Schedules: Integrating Individual and Organizational Needs. Reading, Mass.: Addison-Wesley, 1978.

Commoner, Barry. The Closing Circle: Nature, Man and Technology. New York: Alfred A. Knopf, 1971.

Dickson, Paul. The Future of the Work Place. New York: Weybright and Talley, 1975.

Dumazedier, Joffre. The Sociology of Leisure. New York: Elsevier Scientific, 1974.

Dunnette, Marvin D. Work and Non-Work in the Year 2001. Monterey, Calif.: Brooks, Cole, 1973.

Durkheim, Emile. Division of Labor in Society. Glencoe, Ill.: The Free Press, 1947.

Ellul, Jacques. The Technological Society. New York: Vintage Books, 1964.

Epstein, Joseph. Ambition: The Secret Passion. New York: E. P. Dutton, 1980.

Fleuter, Douglas C. The Work Week Revolution. Reading, Mass.: Addison-Wesley, 1975.

Galbraith, John Kenneth. The Affluent Society. Boston: Houghton-Mifflin, 1958.

_____. Economics and the Public Purpose. Boston: Houghton-Mifflin, 1973.

Gill, Richard T. Economics and the Public Interest. 3d ed. Santa Monica, Calif.: Goodyear, 1976.

Glickman, Albert S., and Zenia Brown. Changing Schedules of Work: Patterns and Implications. Kalamazoo, Mich.: The Upjohn Institute, 1974.

Goldring, Patrick. Multipurpose Man. London: J. M. Dent and Sons, 1973.

de Grazia, Sebastian. Of Time, Work and Leisure. New York: Anchor Books, 1964.

Greiff, Barrie S., and Preston K. Munter. Tradeoffs: Executive, Family and Organizational Life. New York: New American Library, 1980.

Heilbroner, Robert. The Worldly Philosophers: The Lives, Times and Ideas of the Great Economic Thinkers. New York: Simon and Schuster, 1953.

Howe, Louise Kapp, ed. The Future of the Family. New York: Simon and Schuster, 1972.

Janowitz, Morris. The Last Half Century: Societal Change and Politics in America. Chicago: University of Chicago Press, 1978.

Jenkins, Clive, and Barrie Sherman. The Collapse of Work. London: Eyre Methuen, 1979.

Josephson, Eric, and Mary Josephson, eds. Man Alone: Alienation in Modern Society. New York: Dell, 1965.

Kamerman, Sheila B., and Alfred J. Kahn, eds. Family Policy: Government and Families in Fourteen Countries. New York: Columbia University Press, 1979.

Kando, Thomas. Leisure and Popular Culture in Transition. St. Louis: C. V. Mosby, 1975.

Kanter, Rosabeth Moss. Work and Family in the United States: A Critical Review and Agenda for Research and Policy. New York: Russell Sage & Family, 1977.

Kaplan, Max. Leisure: Theory and Policy. New York: John Wiley & Sons, 1975.

Kreps, Juanita. Women and the American Economy in the 80s. Englewood Cliffs, N.J.: Prentice-Hall, 1976.

Larrabee, Eric, and Rolf Meyersohn, eds. Mass Leisure. Glencoe, Ill.: The Free Press, 1958.

LaFargue, Paul. The Right to Be Lazy. Translated by Charles H. Kerr, 1907. New ed. Chicago: Charles H. Kerr, 1975.

Lefkowitz, Bernard. Breaktime: Living Without Work in a Nine-to-Five World. New York: Penguin Books, 1979.

Lenski, George. The Religious Factor. New York: Doubleday, 1963.

Levinson, Harry, Charlton B. Price, Kenneth J. Munden, Harold J. Manol, and Charles M. Solley. Men, Management and Mental Health. Cambridge, Mass.: Harvard University Press, 1962.

Levitan, Sar, and Richard Belous. Shorter Hours, Shorter Weeks: Spreading the Work to Reduce Unemployment. Baltimore: Johns Hopkins University Press, 1977.

Levitan, Sar A., and William B. Johnston. Work Is Here to Stay, Alas. Salt Lake City, Utah: Olympus, 1973.

Linder, Steffan B. The Harried Leisure Class. New York: Columbia University Press, 1970.

Maccoby, Michael. The Gamesman: Winning and Losing the Career Game. New York: Simon and Schuster, 1976.

Meadows, Donella, Dennis Meadows, Jørgen Randers, and William Behren III. The Limits to Growth. New York: Potomac Associates, 1972.

Meakin, David. Man and Work: Literature and Culture in Industrial Society. New York: Holmes & Meier, 1976.

Moore, Wilbert E. Man, Time and Society. New York: John Wiley & Sons, 1963.

Neulinger, John. The Psychology of Leisure: Research Approaches to the Study of Leisure. 2d printing. Springfield, Ill.: Charles Thomas, 1978.

Nollen, Stanley. New Patterns of Work: Highlights of the Literature. Scarsdale, N.Y.: Work in America Institute, 1979.

Nollen, Stanley D., Brenda B. Eddy, and Virginia H. Martin. Permanent Part-Time Employment: The Manager's Perspective. New York: Praeger, 1978.

Nosow, Sigmund, and William H. Forms, eds. Man, Work and Society: A Reader in the Sociology of Occupations. New York: Basic Books, 1962.

Owen, John D. Working Hours. Lexington, Mass.: Lexington Books, 1979.

Pahl, J. M., and R. E. Pahl. Managers and Their Wives: A Study of Career and Family Relationships in the Middle Class. London: Allen Lane and the Penguin Press, 1971.

Peiper, Josef. Leisure: The Basis of Culture. Translated by Alexander Dru. New York: Mentor-Omega Books, 1963.

The Print Project. The Techno/Peasant Survival Manual. New York: Bantam Books, 1980.

Rappaport, Rhona, and Robert Rappaport. Dual-Career Families. London: Harper & Row, 1976.

Robertson, James. The Sane Alternative: A Choice of Futures. St. Paul: River Basin, 1978.

Rosow, Jerome M., ed. The Worker and the Job: Coping with Change. Englewood Cliffs, N.J.: Prentice-Hall, 1974.

Rosow, Jerome, and Clark Kerr, eds. Work in America: The Decade Ahead. New York: D. Van Nostrand, 1979.

Roszak, Theodore. Person/Planet: The Creative Disintegration of Industrial Society. New York: Anchor Books, 1979.

Sale, Kirkpatrick. Human Scale. New York: Coward, McCann & Geoghegan, 1980.

Schumacher, E. F. Small Is Beautiful: Economics as if People Mattered. New York: Harper & Row, 1973.

Silk, Leonard. The Economists. New York: Basic Books, 1976.

Skolnick, Arlene, and Jerome H. Skolnick. Family in Transition. 3d ed. Boston: Little, Brown, 1980.

Smigel, E., ed. Work and Leisure. New Haven: College and University Press, 1963.

Smith, Ralph E., ed. The Subtle Revolution: Women at Work. Washington, D.C.: The Urban Institute, 1979.

Stromberg, Ann H., and Shirley Harkess. Women Working: Theories and Facts in Perspective. Palo Alto, Calif.: Mayfield, 1978.

Tawney, R. W. Religion and the Rise of Capitalism. New York: Harcourt, 1926.

Thurow, Lester. The Zero Sum Society: Distribution and the Possibilities for Economic Change. New York: Basic Books, 1980.

Tilly, Louise, and Joan W. Scott. Women, Work and Family. New York: Holt, Rinehart & Winston, 1978.

Toffler, Alvin. The Third Wave. New York: William Morrow, 1980.

Weber, Max. The Protestant Ethic and the Spirit of Capitalism. London: Geo. Allen and Unwin, 1930.

Woodward, Herbert N. Capitalism Can Survive in a No-Growth Economy. Stamford, Conn.: The Brookdale Press, 1976.

Work in America. Cambridge, Mass.: The MIT Press, 1973.

Young, Michael, and Peter Willmott. The Symmetrical Family. New York: Pantheon Books, 1973.


MONOGRAPHS, PAMPHLETS, AND REPORTS

Catalyst. Flexible Work Schedules. A Catalyst Position Paper. New York: Catalyst, 1973.

_____. Part-Time Social Workers in Public Welfare. New York: Catalyst, 1971.

The Communications Workers of America and The German Marshall Fund of the United States. Innovations in Working Patterns. Washington, D.C.: May 1978.

Exchanging Earnings for Leisure: Findings of an Exploratory National Survey on Work Time Preferences. R. & D. Monograph #79, U.S. Department of Labor, Employment and Training Administration, 1980.

Eyde, Lorraine D. Flexibility through Part-Time Employment of Career Women in the Public Service. Washington, D.C.: U.S. Civil Service Commission, Personnel Research and Development Center, June 1975.

Final Report on the Shared Position Project: Expanded Use of Part-Time Employment. Policy and Standards Division, California State Personnel Board, July 1978, IPA Project #76-21.

Kreps, Juanita. Lifetime Allocation of Work and Leisure. Department of Health, Education, and Welfare, Social Security Administration, Office of Research Statistics, 1968.

Leisure Sharing. Hearing of the Select Committee on Investment Priorities and Objectives, California State Senate, San Francisco, California, November 1, 1977.

Life Cycle Planning: New Strategies for Education, Work and Retirement. Summary of National Conference, April 20-22, 1977, Washington, D.C., Center for Policy Process.

Mead, Margaret. The Changing Cultural Patterns of Work and Leisure. Washington, D.C., Department of Labor, Manpower Administration, 1967.

Menefee, John Alsworth. "The Economics of Leisure: The Evolution of the Leisure-Labor Tradeoff in Economic Doctrines." Doctoral dissertation, Duke University, Department of Economics, 1974.

New Patterns for Working Time. International Conference on New Patterns for Working Time, Paris, Organization for Economic Cooperation and Development, 1973.

New Ways to Work. Reduced Work Time Options: A Selected Bibliography. San Francisco: New Ways to Work, 1981.

Nollen, Stanley D., Brenda B. Eddy, and Virginia H. Martin. Permanent Part-Time Employment: The Manager's Perspective. Employment and Training Administration, Washington, D.C., Office of Research and Development, May 1977.

Part-Time Employment in HEW. Personnel Pamphlet Series No. 5. Washington, D.C.: U.S. Government Printing Office, August 1978.

The Part-Time Employment Pilot Program. Report to the Governor and the Legislature of the State of California, California Department of Motor Vehicles, January 1979.

Ramos, Alberto Guerreiro. "A Critique of Modern Reason." Unpublished Paper, University of Southern California.

Robinson, David. Alternative Work Patterns: Changing Approaches to Work Scheduling. Work in America Reports, 1976.

State of Wisconsin. Project JOIN Final Report. Madison, Wisc.: Department of Employee Relations, 1979.

Stewart, Cheryl, Joanne Kennedy, Christine Sierra, and Charles Gossett. Job Sharing in Municipal Government: A Case Study in the City of Palo Alto, California. Action Research Liaison Office, Stanford University, 1975.

U.S., Civil Service Commission, Bureau of Policy and Standards. Flexitime. Washington, D.C.: U.S. Government Printing Office, May 1974.

U.S., Congress. Committee on Labor and Public Welfare, Subcommittee on Employment, Poverty and Migratory Labor. 94th Cong., 2d sess., 1976. Changing Patterns of Work in America, Hearing, April 7 and 8.

Work Time and Employment: A Conference Report, A Special Report to the National Commission for Manpower Policy, Special Report No. 28, October 1978.

# INDEX

adapters, 75, 95, 116, 117, 121, 122, 125, 132, 134
alternative work pattern, 5, 10, 18, 142, 144
Aristotle, 45, 58, 141
audio mail, 25

Bednarzik, Robert, 6
benefits, 144, 147, 148, 152, 155, 161; disability, 32; flexible, 11, 151, 156, 162; fringe, 32, 34, 51, 56, 102, 105, 149, 150, 151, 159, 160
Boulding, Kenneth, 21
breadwinner model, 31, 32-33, 34, 35, 38, 54, 111, 161
Breit, Miranda, 61
Burns, Scott, 43, 66

Calvin, John, 53
capitalism, 19
career: definition of, 12, 35
careerism, 36
catalyst, 142, 143, 144, 152, 153
central life interest, 132
child care, 41-42, 43-44
circular-traditional time, 2-3
Club of Rome, the, 20, 21
collective bargaining, 5, 11, 32
compensation, 18, 32
compressed work time, 10, 18
contracts: explicit, 111, 114; implicit, 106; psychological, 85, 115

corporate wives, 36-37, 38

dual career: families, 8, 30, 34, 35, 37-39, 43, 46, 108, 116, 121, 122, 124, 161; wives, 30
Dubin, Robert, 61-62, 63, 132
Durkheim, Emile, 54

economies, 64
Eddy, Brenda, 144
employment policy, 9, 18, 27, 31
employment-population ratio, 22
Employment Retirement Income Security Act (ERISA) of 1974, 151
entropy, 20
exchange economy, 21, 26, 53, 160
expressive needs, 51-52, 57

Fair Labor Standards Act of 1938, 5
family policy, 9, 18, 29, 31
Federal Employees Part-Time Career Employment Act of 1978, 147
flexible life planning, 11
Flexitime, 10, 18, 161
full time, 5-7, 9, 27, 33, 34, 41, 43, 44, 46-47, 75, 77, 80, 88, 102-03, 107, 109-10, 111-12, 113-14,

181

# ABOUT THE AUTHOR

ANN HARRIMAN is Associate Professor of Organizational Behavior in the School of Business and Public Administration at California State University, Sacramento.

Dr. Harriman holds a B.S. in Business Administration from University of California, Berkeley, an M.B.A. from California State University, Sacramento, and an M.P.A. and D.P.A. from the University of Southern California.